Relevance of Savarkar Today

Relevance of Savarkar Today

Dr. Ashok Modak

Editors

Prof. Narayan Gune
Prof. Prabhakar Nankar

Translated by

Prof. Shirish Sahasrabudhe

PRABHAT
PRAKASHAN

Published by
PRABHAT PRAKASHAN PVT. LTD.
4/19 Asaf Ali Road,
New Delhi-110 002 (INDIA)
e-mail: prabhatbooks@gmail.com

ISBN 978-93-90923-56-4
RELEVANCE OF SAVARKAR TODAY
by Dr. Ashok Modak

Edition
2025

Price
₹ 400.00 (Rupees Four Hundred only)

Printed at
R-Tech Offset Printers, Delhi

Dedicated with deep reverence
to the pious memory of
Swatantryaveer Vinayak Damodar Savarkar
Great son of Mother India
Ardent patriot and
Priest of nationalism
Inspiration to intense revolutionaries
Genuine social reformer,
endorsing scientific world-view

—Dr. Ashok Modak, Author
—Prof. Narayan Gune, Editor
—Prof. Prabhakar Nankar, Editor

Swatantryaveer Savarkar

Sadhyachya Sandarbhat
Release of the Third Edition
At the hands of hon. Shri Bhagat Singhji Koshyari, Governor of Maharashtra

It is our great fortune that the third edition of our original book in Marathi titled **Swatantryaveer Savarkar: Sadhyachya Sandarbhat** is being released at the auspicious hands of Hon. Shri Bhagat Singh Koshyari, Governor of Maharashtra. Respected Shri Koshyariji served the state of Uttarakhand as its Chief Minister exceedingly well. He is now a much-liked and popular Governor of Maharashtra. He bears in his heart a special affinity towards Veer Savarkar. We are delighted that our book on the Savarkar school of thoughts is being released by such a grand personality on the auspicious day of 7th February, 2020.

In the pre-independence ear, the so-called progressive liberal leaders used to feel gratified in taking an ostrich-like approach to the issues related to Muslims. Their popular concepts were like "These issues were created by the British rulers. The solution lies in majority Hinuds abandoning their Hindutva and embracing an identity as Hindi people. They should ignore the anti-India atrocities of the Muslim League. The should overlook plain truths while narrating Indian history. One can go to the extent of describing a phenomenal leader like Chhatrapati Sivaji Maharaj as a misguided patriot/ And they should be willing to compromise on the fronts of the national anthem, the national language and the national flag. This is how Hindus should behave to ensure unity."

In such a vitiate ecosystem, Swatantryaveer Savarkar was probably the only leader defining the philosophy of Hindutva in unequivocal terms. Savarkar was piously possessed by his concept of the resurrection and recreation of India by uniting all the individuals who considered India as their motherland and also their holy land. All such individuals could be called Nationalists. The Hindus, as per his thinking, would certainly be tolerant but would also possess a triumphant mentality. They would not hesitate in displaying anger with what was unholy. They would stick to truths when it came to the Indian history. But at the same time, they would be willing to walk hand-in-hand with all non-Hindus including Muslims. They would be willing to accept the just and fair demands of the Muslims such as proportional representation in governance. The concept of self-rule (Swarajya) as envisaged by Savarkar, included and welcomed followers of all sects and groups. In that sense, it was Savarkar's polity which was truly secular.

Unfortunately, Savarkar was then completely ignored. In the post-independence period, Savarkar continued to present truly nationalist thinking in very clear terms. But even then, he was cold-shouldered. After his demise, several so-called liberal and progressive intellectuals vied with each other in hurling insults at Savarkar.

The parliamentary elections of 2014, however, led to a miracle. Majority of the voters realised that artificial and ambiguous thinking about the nation and nationality had resulted in huge losses not only to Hindus but also to Muslims. The election results came as a pleasant surprise. The pro-Hindutva candidates were elected by large margins. To top this success came its sequel, in an enlarged form, in 2019 elections. At present, Government of India is getting passed several laws and regulations which will prove strongly beneficial to the national well-being. Rulers of the Bhartiya Janata Party are giving fair justice to the Savarkar doctrine through such laws and regulations. For example, the reforms in citizenship-related laws will facilitate the persecuted minorities who migrated from Afghanistan, Bangladesh and Pakistan into India, seeking asylum. Such persons can now hope to be finally welcomed into India. It is again a pleasant surprise that many Muslim gentlemen have come forward to deeply appreciate the changes in the citizenship laws. Some notable examples are: the incumbent governor of Kerala Mr. Arif Mohammad Khan and the Vice Chancellor of the Urdu University of Hyderabad Professor Feroz Bakht Ahmed. It is now a writing on the wall that a magnificent temple of Prabhu Ramachandra will be constructed on the Ram Janmabhoomi in Ayodhya.

The third edition of the Marathi book 'Swatantryaveer Savarkar: Sadhyachya Sandarbhat' is getting published on this golden backdrop. The dreams of Swatantryaveer Savarkar are being brought to life. We thank the honourable Governor of Maharashtra Shri. Bhagat Singh Koshyari for his blessings to this book. We have also received best wishes from Devendra Fadnavis, the former Chief Minister of Maharashtra and precious assistance from Maharashtra Seva Sangh, Mulund, Mumbai.

This first-ever edition of the original book in Marathi was released by hon. Shri Renga Hari, a veteran member of the Rashtriya Swayamsevak Sangh, in December 2017.

We had then received substantial encouragement from Savarkar Darshan Pratishthan, an institution built by (late) Shri Sudhir Phadke, well known musician and an activist-turned-scholar who was a devotee of Savarkar. We are thankful to our friend Shri. Ravindra Sathe, Secretary of Savarkar Darshan Pratishthan, to Shri Vinayak Joglekar who helped us include good maps in this book and the Shri Arun Phadke, who proof-checked the first Marathi edition in spite of ill health. All the three original Marathi editions were published by Shri Rutuparna Kulkarni of Continental Prakashan. We deeply appreciate his efforts.

We sincerely believe that non-Marathi readers will heartily welcome this first edition in English in the same manner as Marathi readers welcomed three editions so far.

—Dr. Ashok Madak

—Prof. Narayan Gune

—Prof. Prabhakar Nankar

Contents

Sequence of Maps

Brief Life Sketch

Vinayak Damodar Savarkar (Swatantryaveer Savarkar)
(28th May, 1883 to 26th February, 1966)

He was the one who dedicated to the nation's cause every moment of his life. He devoted every drop of blood in his body at the sacred altar of his nation. As a man of letters, he could easily relate himself to the tradition of Maharshi Vyas and Valmiki. Like Rishi Dadhichi, he offered to sacrifice even his bones in the line of defending the nation. At one and the same time, he was an intense patriot, a fire-brand revolutionary, an author with a glowing talent, a soft-hearted poet, a dramatist, a historian, an eloquent orator and a practising social reformer. All these attributes befit Swatantryaveer Vinayak Damodar Savarkar whose life displayed tremendous glory, like a rainbow...!

- **28th May 1883:** Savarkar was born at Bhagur in Nashik district of Maharashtra.
- **1898:** Still a teenager, Savarkar took the oath of starting an armed struggle to set India free from the British rule.
- **1903:** Composed his famed hymn to Goddess of Freedom, *Jayostu tey,* when he was merely 20 years old.
- **1905:** Torched imported clothing to fire as a protest

and awareness campaign, while still a student at Fergusson College, Pune.

- **1906:** Left for England with the blessings of Lokmanya Tilak. There he tried to unite Indians in support of India's struggle for independence. Published the history of the 1857 War of Independence and sent copies secretly into India. This inspired many a patriot for revolution.
- **1909:** Although Savarkar passed his exam for the degree of a Barrister, the British government refused to grant him the title. Meanwhile, Anant Kanhere, a revolutionary, killed Jackson, the Collector of Nashik with the pistol sent by Savarkar from London.
- **1910:** Arrested at London. Tried to escape near French port Marseille. Was sentenced with two back-to-back life imprisonments (1910-1960) and sent to Andaman. Despite suffering intense hardships there, wrote his famous epic *'Kamala'* on the walls of the cellular jail.
- **1924:** Was released from Andaman jail on certain terms. Stayed at Ratnagiri on condition not to enter politics. Savarkar therefore strived for social reforms, particularly eradication of untouchability. Created public awareness despite opposition, by organising Conference for eradication of untouchability, Conference of Mahar community and Movement for all Hindus to break bread together.
- **1937:** Following complete release from captivity, assumed President's post in Hindu Maha Sabha.
- **1938:** Chaired Akhil Bharatiya Marathi Sahitya Sammelan (Literary Conclave).

- **1940:** Historic meeting between Subhash Chandra Bose and Savarkar.
- **1943:** Chaired Akhil Bharatiya Marathi Natya Sammelan (Conclave of theatre persons).
- **1952:** Dropped the final curtain on his revolutionary organisation Abhinav Bharat.
- **26 February 1966:** Embraced death by shunning food and beverage intake.

अनादि मी अनंत मी अवध्य मी भला
मारिल रिपु जगति असा कवण जन्मला

—स्वा. सावरकर

(I am the reflection of the eternal, the infinite and the endless....

An enemy who would finish me has just not been born!)

—Savarkar

Introduction

First Edition

The parliamentary elections of 2014 brought about an unprecedented revolution. Three years passed and voters in Uttar Pradesh (UP) and five more states firmly resolved to strengthen this revolution. As a result, the Bharatiya Janata Party (BJP) emerged victorious in six assembly elections and established its governments in these states. This signified an important change in the psyche of the Indian citizens. Veer Savarkar had ardently desired such a quantum change in the psychological make-up of Hindus and Indians. His ideals touched the souls of Indians 80 years after he voiced them in 1937. This heralded the transformation of Uttar Pradesh from a land of issues to that of solutions.

It also happened in 2017 that the then Defence Minister, Nirmala Sitharaman, camped on the islands of Andaman and Nicobar on the occasion of Diwali, in clear recognition of the significant position of the 'Look East Act East' policy in the foreign affairs of India. Her intention was to study the importance of the islands from the geo-strategic point of view. Swatantryaveer Savarkar, the seer, while stepping in Andaman as a prisoner of the British in the year 1911, had envisioned a strategy. Even under those circumstances, he had expressed his desire that Andaman should become the site of a naval fortress so that it could resist and repulse aggression by any enemy's navy coming from the East. We remembered this incident. That is why, in the first edition of this book, we tried to spell the transitions in the external affairs policy of the Modi government from Savarkar's viewpoint. Coincidentally, it happened at the same time when the Travancore Devaswom Board in Kerala appointed five Dalit youths as official priests in five temples of the state. Long ago, Savarkar had made a yeoman endeavour to persuade the Indians to obliterate all age-old and outdated traditions and drop the seven fetters that bound Indians into divided entities. We, therefore, realised that the decision of the Travancore Devaswom Board must have really appeased the soul of Savarkar and so we took up the writing of the first edition. This was the background of the first edition of the book entitled, *Relevance of Savarkar Today*.

Second Edition

Before the release of the second edition in January 2019, the BJP faced a defeat in the assembly elections in three Hindi heartland states–Rajasthan, Madhya Pradesh and Chhattisgarh. But it may be noted that during the entire period of election campaigning, the so-called secular parties had to embrace soft Hindutva. Even Rahul Gandhi, the then President of the Congress party, visited a number of temples as an election strategy to woo Hindu voters. This demonstrated that though the BJP as a political party may not have succeeded to the expected extent, the amazing relevance of the resurrecting philosophy of Veer Savarkar continued to ignite the Indian psyche.

The presentation in the second edition on Savarkar's

thoughts was divided into 25 sections. The first sub-section of each section was titled 'Thus Spoke Swatantryaveer Savarkar' which extensively quoted Savarkar's views. Subsequently, the current situation was defined and analysed in the light of the views expressed by Savarkar. In the end, the responses of some leading thinkers to Savarkar's philosophy were presented. It seems that this three-dimensional format appealed to the readers, as this edition was lapped up within six months from its release.

Third Edition

When we now present to our readers this third edition of our original Marathi book, we naturally feel delighted. When the first edition was published in December 2017, six months had passed after the declaration of the results of the assembly elections in Uttar Pradesh. The BJP won with a decisive majority and established its own government in Lucknow under the leadership of Yogi Adityanath.

Appeasement of minorities has always been the pivotal point of the overall policy of the secular parties, right from the good old days when Congress took it upon itself to foster the Khilafat movement. Surprisingly, the majority of voters also continued to sing hymns in praise of these secular parties. The secular coterie had made it its favourite hobby to ignore and often attack Hindu religion, philosophy and culture. The BJP astonishingly ventured into abdicating this secular appeasement. It was a pleasant surprise to find that the voters in Uttar Pradesh voted generously for BJP candidates. Savarkar had appealed as early as 1937 that the Indian voters should make it a point to vote for pro-Hindutva candidates. It was after 80 long years that the voters realised the importance of his words and adopted his doctrine in the elections.

Regional nationalism was trumpeted in India right from 1857. For the next eight decades, everybody kept hearing the thunderous sound of this thinking. Although the bitter pangs of the partition of our motherland were experienced in 1947 and continue to hurt as a festering sore, it did not deter the secularists from blowing the bugle of regional nationalism. Even after what happened in Ayodhya and after the 21st century dawned, the basic tenets of the voters' thinking were not changing. This change started happening only after 2014.

On this background, it is worth analysing the antecedents of the third edition published in 2019. Five years have gone by since the 2014 elections and five years ago, Narendra Modi entered the Parliament for the first time as the Prime Minister. The vote share earned by BJP under his leadership in 2014 could be described as the outcome of negative voting by a large proportion of the population fatigued with 10 years of Congress misrule. In 2019, however, there was no doubt over giving one chance to the new rulers. The anti-incumbency factor had severely damaged the prospects of the Congress party under the leadership of Prime Minister Manmohan Singh. In 2019, claimed the secularists that the tables would turn in their favour. The anti-incumbency factor, the secular leaders claimed, would now work against Narendra Modi and his pro-Hindutva party. If all secularist parties were to join hands and muster the support of the downtrodden and the exploited, they could easily trounce the so-called communal, extremist and regressive pro-Hindutva forces, was the optimistic refrain of the secular parties. But then, the results of the 2019 parliamentary polls proved them awfully wrong. The third edition of our original book in Marathi is being released on this backdrop. Several thinkers have commented on how this miracle happened through the ballot box. We have included their analysis in this third revised edition. We have also included an analysis of the poll results and the current challenges before our nation, in the light of the 25 thoughts expressed by Swatantryaveer Savarkar. We have also considered the views of several experts.

All of us have to shoulder the responsibility of creating a new India, strong, able and rich, as dreamt by Swatantryaveer Savarkar. A political and social ecosystem conducive to the realisation of his dreams has already been created. We firmly believe that lovers of nationalist thinker Savarkar will take up the cause of creating a new India.

We thank Mr. Hemant Sardesai for newly designing an appropriate cover for the third edition.

—Dr. Ashok Modak
—Prof. Narayan Gune
—Prof. Prabhakar Nankar

The Triumph of Savarkar's Thinking

When the second term of the Narendra Modi government began in May 2019, several thinkers and political commentators acknowledged the fact in unequivocal terms that the voters had strongly supported the BJP in the light of the achievements made during the first term of the Modi government.

Let us take the example of Ms. Shobhaa De, who by no means is a pro-Hindutva author. But she also candidly acknowledged that the predictions of secular and progressive thinkers like her went haywire, since they had failed to gauge the voters' psyche. Here is a quote from her article:

'I am still struggling for an answer. We were so sure about our own feelings of self-righteous outrage at all that was abhorrent, we totally forgot there was a gigantic Hindustan our there which thought differently... We had shared our sentiments openly... and waited for this 'things' to end. And 'normal' life to resume. Very very dumb of us, I have to admit! Because while we were in a la la land, the asli Hindustani was gearing up for D-Day. And that Hindustani had zero ambiguities and certainly no angst. He/she voted and claimed the space we imagined was exclusively ours.

And this is the Hindustan we have today.'

(How liberals living in la la land misread the 'asli Hindustani', *Times of India*, May 26th, 2019)

Shobhaa De was by no means alone. A large number of other journalists and thinkers also concluded that the election results were a clear endorsement by the citizens of India on the pro-Hindutva policies of BJP.

Remembering the Savarkar Doctrine

Narendra Modi became the Prime Minister for the second time and BJP started its second term in power. The immediate effect was that policies and programmes were initiated over which the earlier governments had dithered for a good 70 years after Independence. Be it the issue of triple *talaq* or abrogation of Article 370, the Modi government started hitting sixers all the way. This was clearly perceived as a victory for Savarkar's doctrine. Savarkar and his followers had been requesting every incumbent government to desist from discriminating between the Hindu and non-Hindu citizens of India. They had appealed to the successive governments to free Muslim women from the barbed fetters of triple *talaq* and to set Kashmir free from the controversial Article 370. The common people of India are therefore happy that Savarkar's dreams are being fulfilled and India is becoming increasingly unified and united as a nation. The common masses find this progress worth rejoicing. However, a few progressive liberals have rushed ahead to criticise the government for implementing the Savarkar doctrine and for thereby creating problems for the country. To cite an illustration, refer to the article by Neeta Chandihok, published in the newspaper, *The Hindu* in its issue dated August 5th, 2019 and titled 'A Political Re-invention in a Moment of Crisis'. We can also quote as another example the interview of Aijaz Ahmed, a Leftist thinker, published by *The Frontline* fortnightly in its issue of August 2nd, 2019. Vaibhav Purandare, a journalist writing for *Hindustan Times* has given vent on August 23rd, 2019 to his hatred of Savarkar. He stated that Modi and Shah stood haunted by the ghost of Savarkar. In conclusion, it cannot be ignored that though five decades and more have passed since the demise of Veer Savarkar, there is no abatement in the malignant and malafide campaign by the so-called secularists to malign the image of Veer Savarkar.

Opponents Concede...

It has become evident that the enthusiastic youths, both girls and boys, who were first-time voters in the new millennium, have bid goodbye to synthetic and unnatural progressive liberalism. This is the first message that emerges from the voting pattern of the 2019 General Elections. The second is that henceforth only such political parties which espouse the cause of a confident and triumphant India will succeed. This has become crystal clear. The third conclusion is that women journalists, such as Shobhaa De, Tavleen Singh and others have also changed their tune and come forth to support the cause of Hindutva. Here are excerpts from the print media. In her article in *Times of India* dated August 18th, 2019, Shobhaa De writes, 'while the Foreign Minister of Pakistan has warned Pakistani citizens not to live in a fool's paradise, the present rulers in India are expressing a confidence that Kashmir was, is and will continue to be the paradise on Earth.. this year Diwali in India will surely shower pleasures.' This way, those who until now were predicting the doomsday, have now changed their tune to sing that the leadership of Modi will lead to some good news. The height of change is that several

Muslim countries of the world are supporting India and the Modi government, instead of Pakistan. That is why some Congress leaders, like Abhishek Singhvi, Jairam Ramesh and Shashi Tharoor have appealed to their partymen to desist from describing Modi as a devil.

Savarkar Doctrine Supports Democracy

Times are changing. While Swatantryaveer Savarkar and his philosophy are constantly under attack from the so-called secularists, Modi and Shah vouch that they are their guiding lights. In their eyes, Savarkar's doctrine is navigating India towards its eventual rise. Prof. Sheshrao More has authored a book titled, *The Assassination of Gandhi and the Defamation of Savarkar*, in Marathi and it is currently the talk of the town. He has clarified therein, with proven evidence, that Veer Savarkar had absolutely nothing to do with Gandhiji's assassination. In fact, assassin Nathuram Godse was an ardent critic of Savarkar. Whereas Savarkar had shown complete willingness to co-operate with the Nehru government in 1947 in the larger interest of India, the Congress government was only too eager to level unholy charges against him and put him behind bars. That is why the Congress government sinned twice by arresting Savarkar twice and keeping him in prison in post-Independence India. In spite of this, Veer Savarkar's speeches were always in consonance with democracy and his conduct also was in keeping with the Indian constitution. Savarkar never spoke ill of Gandhiji or Pandit Nehru. Thus states Sheshrao More: 'In the words of Barrister P.R. Das, the counsel for Savarkar in the court of law, the police confiscated over 10,000 documents from Savarkar Sadan, but did not find even a single word that expressed a foul sentiment about Gandhiji.' (pp. 216-217).

The contrast is absolutely apparent. On the one hand, Savarkar conducted himself in a highly dignified manner in perfect cohesion with the democratic traditions, on the other, the so-called secularists even today engage in his character assassination, using highly indecent expressions that reflect their negative mindset.

Public Welfare is the Best Goal

Swatantryaveer Savarkar toiled all his life for the independence and upliftment of his motherland. He put up with inhumanly gory physical and mental torture during his imprisonment in the infamous Cellular Jail of Andaman. Later, several times he had to swim against the current. For him, the guiding principle was the Sanskrit saying, 'वरं जनहितं ध्येयम्, केवला न जनस्तुति' (public welfare is the noblest objective, not just public praise!) In keeping with it, he walked through fire. He also tolerated with equanimity the shameless attacks from those for whom he had to confront hell! He continued to weather all these storms throughout his life.

Is there any single freedom fighter who had to undergo such nerve-racking physical and psychological torture as Savarkar did? It is most unfortunate for us that we ignore the true history and hurl unholy accusations at this chaste soul and that too after so many decades of his death. The false charges levelled against him will cause unlimited pain to any patriot. But it is also an undoubted fact that it is his doctrine of 'Hindutva First' that is now running triumphant throughout the country, heralding the dawn of the resurrection of the glory of this great country!

Consequences of Acceptance of Hindutva

Renowned thinker and journalist Dilip Padgaonkar had written an article in the *Times of India*, commenting on the election results of 2014. He stated that 'India was no more a gullible country divided against itself and infested with mutual jealousy. India of the 21st century is ready to march ahead successfully on the path of development.' Unfortunately, Dilip Padgaonkar is no more. Otherwise it would have been interesting to read yet another appropriate comment coming from his pen on the people's verdict in the 2019 General Elections.

The Journey of Secularist Parties

The so-called secularist parties are not ready to accept the facts. Their affirmed belief was that 'the Third Front formed by the secular parties will ascend to power. BJP, led by Narendra Modi-Amit Shah duo, will bite the dust in these elections.' With this doomsday prediction, the secularist parties entered the campaigning for the 2019 General Elections and what a humiliation they had to face! Prof. Badri Narayan of Govind Ballabh Pant Social Science Institute, Allahabad, in his article in the *Indian Express* dated May 24th, 2019, thus cast a comprehensive focus on the political ecosystem of UP: 'What BJP crafted as a new social equation was a *gathbandhan* of non-Yadav numerically substantial OBC communities, such as Kurmi, Maurya, etc. and most backward castes including Nishad, Bind, Kasera, Kumhar, Tathera, Tamboli. The party also reached out to non-Jatav Dalit castes, such as Musahars, Nut, Kanjar and Kuchbadhiya. The BJP built this social coalition by organising caste conferences of various most backward and non-Jatav Dalit castes while also ensuring that the benefits of schemes like Ujjwala Yojana, Pradhan Mantri Awas Yojana and Mudra reached them.'

BJP reaped rich rewards for all the hard work and strategic steps taken. This meant that the pro-Hindutva people consciously worked to convey to all sections of the society that the real benefits of the development schemes would reach them. Even when the elections were distant, the Swayamsevaks of RSS were occupied single-mindedly with carrying out multidimensional tasks of the Hindu organisation. On the other hand, the voters realised that the pseudo-secularist leaders, like Akhilesh and Mayawati had become active only when the elections drew closer, and their activities basically included malicious and negative propaganda against the pro-Hindutva thought. The main focus of secularist campaigning was directed at stating that the RSS and BJP were interested only in the welfare of the upper castes. But how could the common voter accept this when his or her own experience was quite different? The last five years have proved beyond doubt that only oratory and journalistic writing do not achieve the purpose of influencing the voters or deviating their attention from real issues.

Future Course of Hindu Nation

On May 28th in the year 2014 as well as in 2019, Prime Minister Narendra Modi bowed with great reverence at the portrait of Veer Savarkar in the Parliament. It was to pay his respects on the occasion of the birth anniversary of Veer Savarkar on 28th May. It was an appreciation of the sympathy and brotherhood that Savarkar felt for the common man and which was to be reflected in the governance of the nation. It is our good fortune that clear indications of such a reflection have been received in the last five years or so. They have been recorded even by foreign journalists. Several humane facets of the personality of Veer Savarkar may not be much known to us. When imprisoned in Andaman, he would wash the clothes of ordinary prisoners around him along with his own clothes. While on his way to Andaman and way back, he would easily mingle with the common fellow travellers on the boat. When he was under house arrest at Ratnagiri, Savarkar would gladly befriend numerous brothers and sisters belonging to various Dalit communities. It is only after taking into account these aspects of his persona, we can be convinced that the model for ideal governance in India is expressed in the *Ishawasya Upanishad*, which says, 'कामये दुःखतप्तानाम् प्राणिनाम् आर्तिनाशनम्' (Problems of all unfortunate creatures harassed by the hellfire of miseries should come to an end.) To achieve this, the elite socio-economic class should be generous and liberal to repay the social obligations.

The reputed magazine *Time* published from the US carried an article by journalist Ian Bremmer in its issue dated May 20th, 2019. It contains a very engaging analysis of how the first five years of the Modi government were spent in taking care of the welfare of the common people. The very heading of the article appropriately said, 'India's Best Hope for Economic Reforms'. The following is the gist of the article:

'In the last five years, 300 million Indian citizens have been encouraged to open their savings accounts in banks. These accounts were used by the government to directly deposit the government subsidies payable to these citizens. This put an end effectively to the evil practice of middlemen demanding their share. Since the net of taxation was enlarged, the government treasury has became stronger. The Modi government has succeeded substantially in constructing a wide network of roads and bridges throughout the country. This in turn has helped the transport and delivery of food-grains and other commodities to the relatively neglected communities living in remote corners of the country. Production and distribution of electricity has been widespread during these five years. Again in the same period, cooking gas connections were installed in a large number of villages, replacing the cumbersome traditional method of burning wood or charcoal for cooking food. Many toilets were constructed in the same period under the 'Clean India' movement. A great deal of efforts were also made to improve the health conditions of women, children and others.'

Indian society experienced in the first five years of the Modi government that the pro-Hindutva rulers do not discriminate between Hindus and non-Hindus when it comes to implementation of public welfare schemes. It was also obvious that special schemes, such as interest-free soft loans, were provided to encourage Dalits and Adivasis to become entrepreneurs. Now it is the wish of the people that the re-elected government should take definite steps to reduce unemployment and to put an end to suicides by farmers by strengthening agriculture through loans and subsidies. All would be happy to see India as a land of plenty.

Pro-Hindutva leaders, such as Veer Savarkar, Dr. Hedgewar, Pandit Madan Mohan Malviya and Dr. Syama Prasad Mookherjee had dreamt of an affluent India. It will be a wonderful tribute to these departed leaders if the present rulers of BJP could fulfil their dreams.

Identical Content

The fact that a pro-Hindutva party had romped back to power with a huge success in the Parliamentary elections of 2019 naturally created ripples in the mass media. Several newspapers wrote articles and editorials presenting appropriate and engaging reactions. A quick and coherent recap thereof would easily explain how the 2019 elections completely transformed the face of Indian politics. The major role of the Savarkar doctrine in instituting this transformation will also become clearer through such a review.

Let us begin with newspaper, *The Hindu*. Its comments on the election results as published in its issue of May 24th can be summarised as follows: "Indian voters have endorsed pro-Hindutva nationalism through these election results. In other words, they have put a stamp of their approval on the line of thinking presented by Vinayak Damodar Savarkar almost a century ago. Narendra Modi is the conduit of Savarkar doctrine and he is the chief architect of this transformation. The thinking of the Congress has been relegated to an insignificant corner, while casting away Nehruvian secularism to the periphery of the political arena."

It is a well-known fact that *The Hindu* and many other newspapers towing its line are frontline critics of followers of Hinduism and pro-Hindutva thinking, but the verdict given by Indian voters has been so unequivocal that *The Hindu* had to concede the voters' endorsement of the Savarkar doctrine! *The Hindu* also thought it fit to predict that henceforth the Savarkar doctrine would occupy the centre stage of political thought while the Nehruvian philosophy would have to make do with a peripheral existence.

The editorial of daily *Asian Age* on May 24th acknowledged that Indian voters had clearly supported Modi's thought that India is the stronghold of Hindus. An article by Ashutosh Varshney got published in the newspaper, *Indian Express* of May 27th expressing an identical line of thinking. Readers also saw similar acknowledgement in the editorial of the *Times of India* on May 24th as well as in the article by Neeraja Chaudhary on the editorial page of the same newspaper.

A number of other political experts accepted and expressed that Indian voters had rejected the so-called secularism and embraced pro-Hindutva thought. They also mentioned that it pointed to the significance of Narendra Modi's popularity in 2014 which has been increasing even after his first tenure of five years. That is why the BJP alone garnered more than 300 seats in the Lok Sabha. Most of the political commentators found it astonishing that the pro-Hindutva image of Narendra Modi has been welcomed by the people of India even more, after five years of his prime ministership.

In the pre-Independence era, when sectoral and regional nationalism was equated with Indian nationalism on a large scale, lone voices such as those of Swatantryaveer Savarkar and Dr. Hedgewar upheld the cause of a Hindu nation and Hindufication of Indian polity and society. After over eight decades, the common people of India are saluting their visionary proclamations. This underlines the Indian tradition expressed in the saying सत्यमेव जयते, नानृतम्. Its first half means that truth always triumphs while the second half tells us that untruth or falsehood never wins. In the pre-Independence period, we rejected the fact that India was a predominantly Hindu nation. It was a noble thought to adopt an inclusive approach and usher in non-Hindus as partners along with Hindus in the struggle for Independence. But we went to the extreme of rejecting Hinduism in this endeavour. We forgot the truth that the pro-Hindutva thinking itself is inclusive and is the common thread that amazingly binds together the entire Indian nation.

Savarkar: Perennial Source of Inspiration

Narendra Modi thought it fit to fold his hands and bow before the portrait of Veer Savarkar in the Parliament after his party's victory in the 2014 General Elections. In a sense, the newly elected Prime Minister of India dedicated his success to the perennial source of inspiration called Savarkar! What a grand coincidence! On December 30th, 2018, he visited the erstwhile Cellular Jail on the Andaman Island. With moist eyes, he remembered Netaji Subhash Chandra Bose and visited the cell where Veer Savarkar had been kept imprisoned. He sat in front of the portrait of Veer Savarkar in that cell in the posture of '*dhyan*' for some time. The lesson that he wanted to imbibe from Savarkar was that neither should success intoxicate us nor our failures frustrate us. This is the inspiration that Narendra bhai drew while sitting in *padmasana* at that holy spot.

—Dr. Ashok Modak
—Prof. Narayan Gune
—Prof. Prabhakar Nankar

1

Beseeching Muslims

Thus Spoke Swatantryaveer Savarkar...

It is you who have initiated the Muslims into the belief that the more they demand the more you yield, the more they frown the more you placate, the more they pocket the more you offer, the more thankless they grow the more you crave for their gratitude. Did you not offer them blank cheques? Dr. Munje, Bhai Paramanand and other leaders of the Hindu Mahasabha protested against the Khilafat policy, against the blank cheques, against meaningless 'neither accept nor reject vagaries', while denouncing them all as wicked communalists, and looking down even upon Shivaji and Maharana Pratap as misguided patriots, because they conquered by the sword while you projected yourself as new messiahs who had come to conquer by love alone, as world guides in direct communications with the inner voice. And now how pitiable it is to find you so desperately search for guidance to appease and win over the Muslims by love alone! That how embarrassing it was that you had to stand imploring at the gates of all the British Governors and the Viceroys to lend you a helping hand. (HTTPS://www.savarkarsmarak.com/activityimages/Hindurashtra%20 Darshan.pdf pp, 73-74)

Current Situation and Analysis

Among the six state elections that we mentioned earlier, the most noteworthy was the BJP victory in Uttar Pradesh (UP), a state with huge expanse of land that is responsible for shaping the national politics of the country. That is why when the BJP won 325 seats out of the total 403 seats of the state assembly, thereby winning 81 per cent seats, the whole country was held aghast. The image of BJP as a staunch pro-Hindutva party received a boost from a state where 19 per cent of the voters are Muslims. Hence traditionally it was the Muslim voters who decided as to who should rule the state. That was why everybody was astonished at the massive victory earned by BJP in UP. The Muslims here had always held the veto power, right since the pre-Independence era. The Hindu society was disorganised. The dominant self-identity that Hindus espoused was not religious, but based on castes, sub-castes, languages/ dialects and religious sects. As a result, 85 per cent Hindu population was divided whereas 15 per cent Muslims were organised, unified and aware. On this background, the minority could dictate terms to the majority. The Muslims as minority citizens kept on placing tough demands in front of the majority. Leaders of the majority went on conceding these demands, ultimately resulting in the Partition of the country. Pakistan cut off the northwestern and eastern parts of India. In spite of this, the Hindu society continued to be divided, meekly accepting the veto power of the Muslims who played a decisive role in successive State and central-level elections. Terms like secularism and progressivism actually glorified the appeasement of minorities, especially that of the Muslims. This practice continued for several decades after Independence.

The Lok Sabha election of 2014 severely blasted the established practices that wore the garb of secularism and progressivism. Voters taught a tough lesson to the so-called secular parties. The assembly elections of 2017 were a carbon copy of the 2014 Lok Sabha election results. A glance at the characteristics of the assembly elections will easily underline the importance of remembering Savarkar.

1. Muslims' Veto Power Proved Ineffective

The BJP did not give election ticket to a single Muslim in UP. When some journalist questioned this, Amit Shah, the then BJP president counterquestioned, "Many other parties have given disproportionately high representation to Muslims. How is that justified?" Narendra Modi explained with evidence as to how the Akhilesh Yadav government had been partisan towards the Muslims and neglected the interests of Hindus. In conclusion, BJP made it the pivotal point of its propaganda that Hindus had been discriminated against and ignored due to the mockery of secularism prevailing in the state so far. Voters elected the BJP candidates by large margins. This simply meant that the so-called veto power of the Muslims had proved to be ineffectual.

2. Rejecting Casteist Voting Patterns

All the elections in Independent India were marked by caste-based politics played by different political parties. Candidates used to be fixed on the basis of dominant castes or sub-castes in the respective constituencies. Yadavs and Jatavs are two dominant communities in UP. Akhilesh Yadav and Mayawati chose their candidates by traditional thinking based on dominant castes. The elections led to a miracle.

Voters who used to vote on the basis of the caste and subcaste of the candidates in the past, threw such small-minded considerations to the winds and supported BJP by voting en masse. A three-member committee comprising Nilanjan Sarkar, Bhanu Joshi and Ashish Ranjan travelled across the length and breadth of UP during the election campaigning period, on behalf of the Centre for Policy Research, New Delhi. They interacted with a large number of voters and published an article on the basis of this survey in the newspaper, *The Hindu* of March 14th, 2017. The following sentence in it is noteworthy: 'The popular view of BJP, in our survey, was that of a caste-blind party!' In conclusion, Mayawati and Akhilesh Yadav made their parties go after conventional narrow casteist politics while BJP underlined Hindutva and ignored such parochial caste-based politics.

3. Endorsement of Decisions of Two-and-a-half Years

After the 2014 elections, Narendra Modi entered the Parliament for the first time. When the Assembly elections in six states were announced, the new government of Modi had completed two-and-a-half years. It meant that he did not enjoy the advantage of a clean slate. He had already conducted the risky experiment of demonetisation, and the Opposition parties were quick to vouch that voters would teach BJP a lesson. It was really amazing how voters proved these doomsday predictions wrong. In other words, the voters conveyed their endorsement of the policies of Modi government through the ballot-box.

Development of All, Faith of All

The voters also took into account some facts, such as being a pro-Hindutva party did not mean that BJP was dead against Muslims and other minorities. The public noted that many trustworthy leaders of minorities were already members of the BJP, whereas some other parties had presented Muslim candidates who were of questionable traits and dubious character. For example, Bahujan Samaj Party of Ms. Mayawati fielded the brother and son of Mukhtar Ansari, a notorious criminal who had already served a jail term on the charges of murder. The *Times of India* in its editorial of January 30th, 2017 heavily criticised such a combination of crime and politics. To conclude, it is just not true that the so-called secular parties had behaved as real care-takers of the minorities. Rather than caring for their welfare and involving them into the decision- making process, these parties used them for their own selfish purposes. On the other hand, the BJP ignored all narrow considerations of caste, sect and religion and adopted welfare schemes to foster genuine public interest. It implemented the 'mantra' '*Sab ka Sath, Sab ka Vikas, Sab ka Vishwas*!'

After its resounding victory in UP, BJP appointed Yogi Adityanath as the Chief Minister of the state. Yogi Adityanath is well known for his staunch adherence to the pro-Hindu line of thinking, for which he has often been at the receiving end from the Opposition parties. It was a general perception that the BJP would select some milder and middle-of-the-line leader to be the Chief Minister to launch a temperate version of Hindutva, but it turned out to be a hardcore Hindu leader, like Yogi Adityanath. Surprisingly in northeast UP, which is the stronghold of Yogi and where he has consistently done a lot of good work in the recent past, several Muslim citizens came forward to certify that UP had got the right man to be the Chief Minister.

We have so far reviewed the general views expressed in the media and the people's reactions after the six state assembly elections and especially after the results of the UP assembly elections. It is important to note that most of these reviews and remarks encourage us to remember what Savarkar had stated many decades ago, if we follow his line of thinking. That is why in the beginning of this section, we had summarised under the heading 'Thus Spoke Veer Savarkar' his views of as early as 1939.

Hindu Stands for Enlightenment

In Bengal, the Communists and workers of Trinamool Congress have been consistently spreading hatred through false and vile anti-Hindu and anti-RSS propaganda. In contrast, supporters of Hindutva have been working towards uniting the society in a quiet but determined manner for the last several years. Naturally, it occurred to the voter king to reconsider his options. Amartya Sen, the reputed economist-turned-political commentator had predicted that chanting the name of Shri Ram would be an utter waste in Bengal. In reality, Bengalis upheld the slogan 'Amar Naam Tomar Naam, Jai Shri Ram Jai Shri Ram', trouncing the age-old red colour slogans of "Amar Naam Tomar Naam Vietnam, Vietnam'! A senior leader from Maharashtra, Sharad Pawar, also had raised a doubt as to 'who will respect the name of Shri Ram, South of the Narmada!' He even went to the extent of propagating at Ayodhya that the demolished mosque should be rebuilt on Ram janmabhoomi! However, the common voters turned such speeches into wild blabbers! Some economist had held Hindutva responsible for the tardy economic progress in India. When Indian economy was growing at a slow pace of 2.5-3 per cent, he had dubbed it as 'Hindu rate of growth!' What he meant was Hindutva was equal to retarded progress. A Marathi writer had also equated Hindutva with disposable scrap material of life! The Indian voter, however, showed each one of them his right place and position!

□

2

Hindu-Muslim Unity

Thus spoke Swatantryaveer Savarkar...

Right in the pre-independence era, Savarkar had asked this question of Congress leaders: "Do Muslims really wish to be united with the Hindus?" Dr. D.N. Gokhale used to say, "Savarkar has always been making tremendous efforts to change the body language and the nature of the Hindus. He wanted Hindus to be brimming with confidence and self-respect. There was a fundamental difference between the attitudes of Congress leaders and Veer Savarkar. Gandhiji assumed that the issue of Muslims did not exist in India. From Savarkar's point of view, this issue not only existed but was becoming more and more complex and grave. Muslim reformer (late) Hamid Dalwai has said in his book, *Muslim Politics in Secular India*: "When Muslims number up to 49 in a hundred, they are supporters of democracy. But as soon as they become 51 per cent, they strongly subscribe to autocracy." In spite of this, Hindus have always wished for unity with Muslims because Hindus by nature are inclusive and tolerant. Savarkar also desired Hindu-Muslim unity, though he knew that it could not be achieved through one-way attraction or through giving extra-ordinary importance to Muslims. He felt that

Muslims also had to feel the need for unity with Hindus. For this to happen, Hindus had to break away from the barriers of castes and sub-castes and follow the dictum 'All Hindus are One!' In the light of this *mantra*, Hindus should begin by becoming organised, united and confident. This was the stance taken by Savarkar.

Current Situation and Analysis

Results of the 2014 General Eelections were a clear signal to the world that Hindus were becoming organised and confident. The assembly elections of 2017 further demonstrated that the level of unity and confidence among the Hindus was on the rise. As a result, the Muslim community had started the process of introspection. Muslim thinkers were now expressing themselves more freely, as they opposed the so-called progressive and socialist parties. Today, some of them are coming forward with testimonials to prove they are genuine pro-Hindutva thinkers. The extent of this process is visible in the articles of Saba Naqvi and Zoya Hasan. Muslim thinkers are also underlining the deficiencies in the Muslim society more fearlessly. 'The feeling of separatism does not help us. India should be united'–a feeling that is gaining ground among the Muslims.

Seniors' Views

1. Yogendra Yadav

A Left-wing leader and activist, Yogendra Yadav is the president of Swaraj India. His analysis is worth mentioning: "The verdict has again exposed the political bankruptcy of non-BJP parties. Social justice by SP and BSP is shown to be nothing but casteism. Secularism is shown to be either pandering to Muslims or keeping them hostage. Socialism has failed to meet the needs and touch the aspirations of the poor. The Opposition is playing simple-minded anti-Modi politics, which does not click with voters. Modi is positive, proactive and aggressive. The Opposition is defensive, reactive and negative. Non-BJP politics needs a fundamental re-orientation. Secular politics needs to connect to our traditions, cultures and languages. Politics of social justice must move beyond caste-based reservations. And we all must recover the legacy of Indian nationalism." (*Times of India*, March 14th, 2017, p. 12).

2. Shiv Visvanathan

'One has to understand that this victory was so total that it was virtually emasculating to the Opposition. Brutally put, it went beyond a capture of votes to a seduction of the imagination. So far, the two great concepts of Indian electoral politics were socialism and secularism. Mr. Modi has rendered them effete. ('Reflection on the Election of Our Time', *The Hindu*, March 15th, 2017, p. 8).

3. Saba Naqvi

'A Yogi Adityanath could not have been elevated to CM of the country's largest state, had there not been a complete hollowing out of secular values...let's recognise that secularism as practiced in India has been reduced to electoral management, that first sees Muslims as a herd and then tries to keep that herd together.

Practitioners of the craft of secular politics have auctioned out the task of delivering the imaginary herd to a bunch of middlemen, all too often clerics or strongmen with criminal antecedents.

The same clerics also have their hand in managing Waqf properties. There are approximately 3,00,000 registered Waqf properties in India on about 4,00,000 acres of land. Many Waqf Boards are repositories of corruption, both petty and large. Yet they get away with it because any demand for scrutiny is described as an attack on Islam. It's all rather pathetic. Indeed a politician such as Mayawati should recognise that her projection of the *mullah*-meat trader-muscleman candidates hurt rather than help a community she so grandiosely set out to represent.'

Saba Naqvi's article also answers the query as to the nature of an all new secular manifesto:

1. Tell the *mullahs* to restrict their activities to the *masjid*. Begin the process of examining the structures of Law Boards and Wakf Boards managed by groups of men guarding their turfs. Get professionals to create a genuine welfare structure for the community.
2. Ask for participation in existing government schemes instead of harping on separate identity that the Constitution guarantees. Build campaigns over economic issues, jobs, small loans, education and not issues such as triple *talaq*.
3. Salvation lies in propagating the many cultural traditions that unite, not those that separate. Take on the conservative views on music, women's rights and freedom. Highlight the pluralist traditions.
4. If someone comes asking for votes on the basis of fear and tells you that Muslims are supposed to be in the frontline of the battle to save secularism, turn around and tell them in that case it may not really be worth saving(*Times of India*, March 21st, 2017, p. 14).

4. Syed Ata Hasnain

This upright army officer retired after doing a great job in the capacity of the commander of the Srinagar camp of the Indian Army. Post retirement, he has written thought-provoking and well-balanced articles in the last few months in various newspapers. For example, General Bipin Rawat, the formal Chief of Staff once went on record telling people of Kashmir to allow Indian Army to neutralise the outsider terrorists working against the interests of Kashmir and India. If some local citizens create obstacles in the course of such Army action, such citizens may be considered as supporters of terrorism or overground workers and dealt with suitably. Though what the General said was logical and practical, the pseudo-secularists in our country created an anti-Rawat storm, alleging that the General viewed all citizens of Kashmir as enemies of the nation. At that time, Commander Syed Ata Hasnain came out unequivocally in defence of General Bipin Rawat. He said in clear terms that 'General Rawat's coming as the Army Chief and his full knowledge and experience of the way it needs to be handled, can be a great force multiplier. General Rawat is a highly experienced officer and thinks in a very balanced manner. His statement pointed towards those few Kashmiri youth who are targeted by false and vilified propaganda of the Islamic State. The General did not hold all Kashmiri citizens as the enemy of the nation.' (*Times of India*, February 17th, 2017, p. 12). Commander Syed Ata Hasnain in his other articles has this to communicate to Indian Muslims:

'They must understand that they enjoy the benefits and rights of full-scale democracy which few of their co-religionists are fortunate to possess or experience across the world. Even as Islam struggles to balance itself in the Middle East and other regions, Indian Muslims are already balanced and must therefore project this to the Islamic world' (*Times of India*, February 16th, 2017, p. 16).

□

3

Majority-Minority

Thus Spoke Swatantryaveer Savarkar

Exactly 83 years ago, in the year 1937, the Hindu community became familiar with the contents of the book, *Hindurashtra Darshan*. Veer Savarkar had given a very clear warning to all the Hindus:

'When the huge majority in a nation kneels and prostrates itself in front of a hostile minority like the Moslems, prays and begs for its help and assistance and continuously vouches of its certain death without it, it will be extremely surprising if that minority community did not sell its assistance and help at the highest obtainable price, if it does not quickly attempt to bring that majority to its end and establish its own political hegemony in that land.' (*Savarkar Vichar Darshan*, p. 141).

Current Situation and Analysis Hindu-Muslim Relations

Swatantryaveer Savarkar always pleaded the case of Hindu Mahasabha. He invariably kept thinking about the well-being and long-term interests of the Hindus. This is because the Congress, the socialist and communist parties were shy of even uttering the word 'Hindu'. Their constant refrain was that Hindus as well as non-Hindus should become 'Hindi'. The stark reality was that non-Hindu citizens were not willing to become 'Hindi'. Muslims, in fact, were prepared to do anything that it took to create a separate nation of Pakistan. As a result, though the Hindus compromised on multiple fronts, such as the national anthem, the national language, national flag and the definition of a nation, the Muslims did not deter even an inch from the objective of separating Pakistan from India. On the one hand, the Muslims were becoming more and more obstinate, on the other, the secularist forces continued with their refrain of surrendering to every demand of the Muslims. In such a scenario, Savarkar and his Hindu Mahasabha had to take the lead to protect the interests of the Hindus. India achieved political Independence on August 15th, 1947, but the secularist leaders continued to be completely haunted by the ghost of appeasement of Muslims. It was only as recently as in 2017 that the assembly elections in Uttar Pradesh afforded an opportunity to BJP to defeat this ghost single-handedly and completely.

Experts' Views

1. Zoya Hasan

A teacher at Jawaharlal Nehru University, Delhi and Council for Social Development, Delhi, Zoya Hasan wrote, 'The strategy of reverse social engineering that Mr. Shah scripted was clearly aimed at mobilising the most backward castes to capture the heartland state. Mr. Modi's assiduous wooing of non-Yadav OBCs and Dalits convinced large sections of them to desert the SP and BSP in the 2014 Lok Sabha election and again in the 2017 assembly elections. No one can match up to the appeal and energy of Mr. Modi when it comes to non-stop election campaigning and the organisational capacity of the RSS when it comes to relentless propaganda and booth management executed in this election by 1.4 lakh booth *samitis*" (*The Hindu*, March 16th, 2017, p. 8).

2. Indian Express

A notable remark: 'The massive BJP win in the UP assembly elections has signalled that the days of inclusive politics are over. Political parties would now be wary of appealing to the Muslim vote, since that could trigger a reverse mobilisation of Hindus. By not fielding a single Muslim candidate for the Vidhan Sabha, the BJP has also signalled that Muslim votes can't influence its winnability. The BJP mobilised voters in its favour by foregrounding development...' (*Indian Express*, March 17th, 2017, p. 15).

Once the election results have endorsed the fact that Hindufication of Indian politics can become successful, secularist Janata Dal leaders have also started presenting the true history of India...It clearly spells a win for the Savarkar line of thinking.

Of course, many thinkers have expressed an anguish that since a pro-Hindutva party, such as BJP has become the nationally dominant political entity, non-Hindus, minorities and especially Muslims will find it extremely difficult to survive in India. Hindus will treat non-Hindus as secondary citizens and children of lesser gods! However, this anxiety is completely non-relevant.

3. Prof. Mohamed Ayyub

Savarkar always counselled his Hindu brothers to beware of Muslims. This advice still holds good. Sometime back, there was a controversy in Aligarh Muslim University regarding the portrait of Muhammad Ali Jinnah. At that time, Prof. Mohammed Ayyub, who teaches at Michigan University in US had argued: 'Jinnah Sahib was a traitor. He had betrayed the Muslims and hence his portrait should have been removed on August 15th, 1947 itself.' The deeper purport of this argument should be keenly understood. 'Muslim League was established in 1906. Its objective was to safeguard the interests of Muslims in India, especially in those provinces where Muslims were in minority. However, Muhammad Ali Jinnah created a separate State called Pakistan out of the provinces wherein Muslims were in majority! In doing so he threw to the winds the interests of the Muslims who were in minority in other provinces.' This is the real argument which Prof. Ayyub has put across in another article later (refer to *The Hindu,* December 27th, 2018). This clearly shows that when the Hindu community was fighting tooth and nail for the Independence of India, the Muslims in India were not fighting for the country's Independence, but were threatening the Hindus for protecting the selfish interests of their own tribe! It is significant that Prof. Ayyub thought it fit to present this argument even after seven decades have gone by since Independence. In such an atmosphere, Savarkar's warning that continuous vigilance only can protect the interests of the Hindus is still relevant. Of course, Savarkar also held as sacred the principle that Hindus, Muslims, Christians and all other religious groups should closely and amicably coexist as friends in India, and that there should be no discrimination against any individual on the basis of colour, class, sect, creed, etc.

4. Harsh Mander

Leaders and ministers of BJP have implemented the true spirit of secularism and have brought to book anyone who has acted against such secularism. It is a pleasant surprise that no political party has tried to use the Godhra violence in Gujarat in 2002 as a weapon in the campaigning in the recent assembly elections, the way it had been used in the past. 16 years ago, Narendrabhai Modi was dubbed by his detractors as '*maut ka saudagar*'. In the present context, this epithet seems to have disappeared. Harsh Mander, a political commentator, has reviewed all the election campaigns from 2014 onwards and has given his own comment as follows: 'After BJP proved that elections can be won on the basis of Hindutva, all anti-BJP parties, including the Congress, had to substantially alter their campaigning strategies for the assembly elections of Gujarat, Karnataka, Madhya Pradesh, Chhattisgarh, Rajasthan, Mizoram and Telangana. None of the parties kept on harping on the tune that the minorities are badly off in India' ('Speak up, Act' in *Indian Express*, December 17th, 2018, p. 11).

□

4

Hindufication of Politics

Thus Spoke Swatantryaveer Savarkar...

We must understand the concept of Hindufication of politics as envisaged by Veer Savarkar. It is essential to bring to the attention of the people how the Savarkar doctrine is relevant and appropriate, even after eight decades, to the present political scenario. The first principle is that in the current political setup, the Hindus should nourish self-confidence and should unite under one umbrella. Secondly, they should abdicate and obliterate parochial politics based on castes and sub-castes and lingual groups. The third principle is that the liberal, inclusive and patriotic Muslims should be treated with a friendly overture. In fact, all non-Hindus should be indianised in brisk steps. The fourth action point is that secularism in its true sense should be implemented. In other words, all of us should worship justice and humanitarian attitude, forgetting the narrow considerations of sects, castes and religions. Savarkar had expressed his goodwill towards Shia Muslims in 1939. Around the same time, in 1937, he had underlined his strategy for obtaining political freedom in these words: 'Henceforth, the Hindu formula for Hindu-Moslem unity is only this–if you come, with you; if you do not, without you and if you oppose, in spite of you–the Hindus will continue to fight for their national freedom as best as they can!'

Current Situation and Analysis

In 2017, 80 years were completed since Savarkar made that historic speech in 1937. In that year, Swatantryaveer Savarkar had been completely set free after undergoing a variety of jail terms for almost 27 years. He then joined the Hindu Mahasabha and the very same year, 1937, he was chosen as the President at the all-India session of the Hindu Mahasabha held in Karnavati (Ahmedabad). In his historic speech, Savarkar proclaimed the necessity for Hindufication of politics. We must quote Dr. D.N. Gokhale here: 'Savarkar wanted to change the body language and the basic nature of the Hindus. Since the year 1857, that is 80 years before 1937, the Indians had readily accepted Hindi nationalism. By 1937, leaders and followers had all adopted Hindi nationalism. A few visionary leaders of the people, such as Dr. Keshav Baliram Hedgewar, were notable exceptions. On this background, Veer Savarkar propounded Hindu nationalism in very clear terms. (D.N. Gokhale, *Hindutva Darshan*, Pune, 1983, p. 26).

Indian Nationalism and Hindu Nationalism

In 1937, Veer Savarkar roared that Hindi nationalism, which had mounted the Hindus since 1857, i.e. for 80 years, was unfair and harmful. 'The true nationalism of India is Hindu nationalism,' he stated emphatically. He was very well aware that he would be swimming against the tide by announcing this and that it may result in lowering his popularity. But still he justified it with evidence regarding the significance of Hindu nationalism. He also followed it up by a repeated message of Hindufication of politics. But the real issue was about changing the basic nature of the Hindus. Such fundamental changes do not take place easily and quickly. Naturally, within 10 years from Savarkar's message, Muslims succeeded in dividing our motherland and creating a separate Pakistan for themselves. Many of them did not feel satisfied even then and hence chanted slogans like, 'We got Pakistan with a smile, now we will fight to capture Hindusthan.' It meant that they wanted entire India to be their fiefdom, as had happened during the peak of the Mughal period. Muslims went on increasing their nuisance value tremendously. But unfortunately, the Hindu leaders of Congress did not learn any lesson from history and did not think it fit to change their core strategy. Congress, Socialist, Communist, Swatantra (independent party): all these parties did not have any qualms in surrendering to the nuisance value of the Muslims. Muslims kept on placing demands after demands and the Hindu leaders fulfilled them one after another, under the misconceived notion of implementing the principles of secularism. Not only that, but they also kept on insisting that in order to prove themselves to be true nationalists, they must take Muslims along with them and hence kept on delivering doses of such pseudo-secular principles to the Hindus. This continued to be the scenario in every election in Independent India.

Elections to six state assemblies were held in the year 2017. BJP could form governments in all the six states. This resulted in almost complete neutralisation of the Congress Party which had been in power at the Centre and in the states for over 65 years since Independence. This victory reminds us of the values espoused by Veer Savarkar during his life-time. He always had to face unfavourable circumstances and clashed with the powers-that-be and their principles. People at large could not accept his thoughts at that time. However, 51 years after his death, the electorate put a stamp of its approval on the Savarkar doctrine. This is the sum and substance of these election results.

As stated earlier, Savarkar and Hedgewar, two great minds, were almost obsessed with bringing about a sea change in the fundamental nature of the tenets of the Hindu society. For several centuries, the Hindus had wrongly treated narrow considerations of caste, creed and languages as the basic principles of Hinduism. This had divided the Hindus. Both these great souls had been anguished with this situation and had nourished the ambition of convincing the Hindus that Hinduism was much bigger than what they had imagined. India, spreading from the Himachal to Kanyakumari, had an organic and inseparable relationship with the Hindus and their religion. It was necessary to make the Hindus aware of their magnificent and wide-ranging legacy and to resurrect in real sense the slogan, 'Bharat Mata ki Jai!' This ambition of these two visionary leaders was fulfilled 80 years after 1937. It is also equally true that during these eight decades, the so-called liberal progressive school of thinking has played a kind of magic on the entire length and breadth of India. We must accept with an open mind that it will take some more time to end the effect of this unholy magic. That the BJP did not get the expected number of seats in three other assembly elections is also a fact. However, it should not be misconstrued as a defeat of the Savarkar doctrine. It is significant that the campaigning for these assembly elections established it clearly that the so-called secular parties, always opposing BJP's preference for Hindu culture, started giving importance to the feelings and emotions of Hindu citizens. The campaigning also made it clear that BJP was out to put an end to the falsified appeasement of minorities, especially the Muslims. That is why the voters could witness the then Congress President,

Rahul Gandhi visiting every major Hindu temple wearing the sacred thread and proclaiming himself to be a devout Hindu! This sudden change, the voters perceived, was limited only to the external appearance and its origin was the political compulsion of getting elected! But more than this facade, one should realise the underlying message that no political leader can afford to ignore or offend the sanctity of the beliefs of the Hindu society in the future.

Seniors' Views

1. Prof. Shiv Visvanathan

'The so-called secularist leaders and their followers,' according to Prof. Shiv Visvanathan, 'kept on taking the initiative to form the Orwellian clubs everywhere,' (*The Hindu*, May 22nd, 2014). One should clarify what an Orwellian Club means. George Orwell, a famous British author of the 20th century, wrote a novel, *Animal Farm*, which became exceedingly popular. It brought out the fallacies of the communist model of society and governance. He depicted how the so-called equality-centric communist pattern enabled the senior leaders and office-bearers of the Communist Party to enjoy special privileges, whereas the common citizens starved. The Communist Party leaders and cadres received more equal treatment than the other equals in the Soviet Union! This was the truth that Orwell brought out pungently. Shiv Visvanathan has named such a club of privileged communist leaders as the 'Orwellian Club'. In India, the analogy works this way: the pseudo-secularists gave too much importance to Muslims and treated them as more equal than others. They also propagated for a long time that providing such perverse privileges contained the essence of Indianness. 80 years of such politics are now over. Such a long time was probably required for so completely changing the character of the typical Hindu mindset. That is why, though the truth of the 'Muslim Orwellian Clubs' got exposed in 2014, three more years were required and finally in 2017, the veto power enjoyed by the Muslims was finally buried in the land blessed by Ganga and Yamuna.

2. Valerian Rodrigues

In the last three years, the present government felicitated several Sufi Muslims. It got connected to many Islamic countries in the Middle East in a very friendly manner. As Chief Minister of UP, Yogi Adityanath chose one Muslim citizen in his ministry. The Central Government started implementing its promise of *'Sab ka Saath, Sab ka Vikas'*. In his article in *The Hindu* of March 30th, 2017, Valerian Rodriguess remarked, 'The Hindutva project has been surreptitiously redefining the Muslim world in this region that has global ramifications.'

3. Suhas Palshikar

Savarkar's notion of the resurrection of entire Hindusthan or India was largely dependent on the political awareness of the Hindu self. Looked from the eyes of Mr. Suhas Palshikar, Narendra Modi is progressing in the light of this notion of Savarkar. Says Palshikar, 'Modi's Hindutva exhorts the followers to become Hindus politically conscious. Conflation between nationalism and Hindutva has been the backbone of the new hegemony.' ('India's Second Dominant Party System', *EPW*, March 25th, 2017, p. 15).

Palshikar informs his readers, 'It has also been the only and first party to win a clear majority since Rajiv Gandhi did so in 1984. Also in the post-Indira Gandhi period,

Modi is the only leader to truly claim mass appeal almost throughout the country. Therefore, as I argued initially in the aftermath of the last parliamentary elections, the coming of Modi's BJP in 2014 marked a shift away from the past quarter of a century. This indeed was a new phase that was commencing in India's competitive politics. (*EPW*, March 25th, 2017) The outcome in UP has again underlined the change–and now it seems that many observers are ready to accept this reality. The present moment is undeniably the moment of the second dominant party system.'

Needless to state that the dominant party has emerged so because the Hindu voter has become politically conscious. Hence the statement of Veer Savarkar has been actually proven true.

4. Gautam Adhikari

When BJP won 81 per cent seats in UP assembly and then elected a staunch pro-Hindu leader Yogi Adityanath as the Chief Minister, some of the progressive thinkers in our country started asking a quation, 'What will happen to Muslim citizens?' Gautam Adhikari wrote an editorial titled 'Clash of Nationalisms' in *Times of India* issue of March 18th, 2017. He writes, 'There seem to be two distinct nationalisms: inclusionary and exclusionary. One symbolises loyalty to a nation that is tolerant, accommodative and open to evolving cultures and mores. The other advocates a nation which must resist diversity and construct an exclusive ethno-religious identity that must be defended against any dilution the other might bring into society.'

5. Prabhat Patnayak

In a lecture delivered in the lecture series in February-March, 2016 at Jawaharlal Nehru University, New Delhi,

Prabhat Patnayak expressed his view thus: 'The nationalism of the RSS, like European nationalism, is intolerant, exclusive and ambitious.'

6. Sagarika Ghose

Perhaps with similar furious fears lurking in her mind, Sagarika Ghose wrote an article titled, 'UP's New Hindu Rashtra must try reaching out to Muslims', in the 19th March, 2017 issue of *Times of India*. She offered to Prime Mminister Narendra Modi an unsolicited advice to appreciate the value of the support of Muslims. The article reminded Modi government of the Hindu empire of Vijayanagar in this manner: 'The size of the UP mandate gives the Prime Minister a unique opportunity. Hindu kingdoms do not necessarily have to be exclusionary. The great 14th-century Vijayanagar empire showed care and benevolence towards all citizens. If 2017 is the dawn of a new Hindu dispensation, the new government has the chance to rise above the violent communal rhetoric (which is the trademark of Adityanath) and move towards a new Hindu-Muslim social contract.'

□

5

Vijaynagar: An Illustration

Thus Spoke Swatantryaveer Savarkar...

In his book *Saha Soneri Paney* (Six Golden Leaves), Savarkar underlined that the ideal set by the Hindu empire of Vijayanagar is still a laudable and replicable model. He writes, 'Though the rulers of Vijayanagar had a 'tit for tat' policy for the invading Muslim armies, the overall policy of the empire was to accommodate all religions and sects. Several foreign travellers have sung the praises of the justice and fairness, valour and richness of the empire of Vijayanagar. One of them, Duarte Barbose, a Portuguese traveller, says, "You can witness groups of people from different states and religions walking the streets of Vijayanagar. The empire attracts several traders and other elite people from various countries. Nobody troubles them in any manner or questions their place of origin, religious sect or national identity. Muslims, Yahudis, Christians or Hindus from other kingdoms: all are equally welcome. However, in the eyes of law, they are all treated as equal and the innocent are protected, while the guilty get punishment" (D.N. Gokhale, *Hindutva Darshan*, 1983, p. 94).

Current Situation and Analysis

After assuming the office of the Prime Minister, Narendra Modi has created a respectable image of India not only among the Indian Muslims but among the Muslims of various countries in the world. Even such countries have given the new India their positive testimonials. And they are quite vocal. They serve as illustrations of the fact that the Modi government is walking along the lines of the erstwhile Hindu empire of Vijayanagar.

It is a fact that Narendra Modi has a special affinity for Swatantryaveer Savarkar, almost to the extent of deep reverence. In 2014, he took the oath as Prime Minister on May 26th and just two days later, May 28th being the birth anniversary of Savarkar, Narendrabhai folded his hands in front of the portrait of Savarkar in the Parliament. Later, on June 11th, 2014, Modi presented to the members of the Parliament some glimpses of Indian history as envisaged by Savarkar. A striking sentence in his speech was, 'It is the mindset of the slavery of 1,200 years that is bogging down us Indians.' Swatantryaveer Savarkar felt and wrote that Edward and Aurangzeb, both were the enemies of Indians. And therefore, replacing Edward with Aurangzeb could never be the objective of the struggle for Independence. To speak the truth, Indian citizens would not feel any allegiance to Aurangzeb. That is why, what was Aurangzeb Road in Delhi for several decades has now acquired a new name: Dr. APJ Abdul Kalam Marg.

Seniors' Views

1. Irfan Habib

This Leftist Muslim thinker feels that the tenure of Aurangzeb in India was praiseworthy, because India's borders had then spread from Kabul to River Tungabhadra!

2. Dr. Rajendra Prasad

The first President of Independent India heartily

welcomed the reconstruction of the Sorati Somnath temple in Junagadh, Gujarat. It was not just 'lip service'. He participated in the function and in the *abhishekam* (sprinkling of holy water on the *pindi* of Bhagwan Shankar, declared to the audience, "Today's *abhishek* (consecration) has cleansed the sins of 1200 years!"

3. Dr. Babasaheb Ambedkar

Dr. Ambedkar, in his speech in the Constituent Assembly of India, said on November 25th, 1949, 'Muhammad-bin-Qasim had attacked India in the year 712. He defeated Raja Dahir of Sindh and usurped his throne. The story of the slavery of India started from then and there.'

4. Pawan Verma

This former bureaucrat-turned-leader of Janata Dal also felt it necessary and appropriate to say that 'at least for 1,000 years India was under the slavery of alien powers and hence many of the original Indian cultural notions, values and practices were destroyed during this long period.' He wrote thus in an article titled 'India's Politics of Fear' in the *Times of India* issue dated April 6th, 2017: 'History has its own serendipities. On 6th December, 1948, exactly 44 years before the demolition of the Babri Masjid, the Constituent Assembly, which drafted our Constitution, was in the throes of a heated discussion on the question of secularism and the new republic. While there was unanimity that India would not be a theocratic State and that secularism did not imply contempt or marginalisation of the religion, Loknath Mishra, a member of the Constituent Assembly from Orissa (who later, in the 1990s, became Governor of Assam) warned that a "secular State is a slippery phrase, a device to bypass the ancient culture of the land... justice demands that the ancient faith and culture of the land should be given a fair deal if not restored to its legitimate place after a thousand years of suppression".' (*Times of India*, April 6th, 2017, p. 14).

□

6

Hindu Nation: Self-made

Thus Spoke Swatantryaveer Savarkar...

While delivering his presidential address at the Kolkata session of Hindu Mahasabha in 1939, Savarkar put forward a very logical analysis. He stated that the Hindu *rashtra* (nation) was not born in opposition to anyone. Therefore Hindu Mahasabha, which is the timely expression of Hindu *rashtra,* was also not born against any other entity. Of course, Hindudom, that is Hindu Mahasabha, has to sometimes take an aggressive stance while sometimes it has to go on the defensive only to keep under leash the pseudo-secularists. Nevertheless, antagonism or hatred has never been the objective of Hindu Mahasabha. (*Selected Wworks of Veer Savarkar*, vol. 4, Chandigarh, 2007, p. 296).

Current Situation and Analysis

The issue of Hindu-Muslim relations should be viewed and elucidated from the point of view of Swatantryaveer Savarkar. Savarkar had clarified beyond doubt that Hindu Mahasabha was not born out of a reactionary process nor was it intended to ignite hatred against Muslims or other non-Hindus.

The policy of the loyalists to Hindutva towards non-Hindus is highly comprehensive and balanced. In his presidential address at the 1938 session of the Hindu Mahasabha at Nagpur, Savarkar made it absolutely clear that Bharatvarsh or Hindu *rashtra* has had a highly natural birth and rise. Its further development has also been an organic process. Unfortunately Muslims and some Christian citizens could not identify themselves with the national life-course of India. They wanted to establish and run their own fiefdoms and then started asking for a heavy price, say, that of veto power, to join the national stream of life. Savarkar unequivocally declined to pay the price of awarding veto power to non-Hindus. That is the reason why even today, the so-called progressive liberals treat Savarkar as an outcast.

Swatantryaveer Savarkar was speaking with due confidence when he said that this nation had been constructed on the strong foundation of the *Vedas* and *Upanishads,* much before even the advent of Islam or Christianity. Even today this nation is brimming with life because of its continuing thread of memory that relates it to times immemorial. Swami Vivekananda and Mahatma Gandhi presented to us the lives and times of Bhakta Prahlad, Raja Harishchandra, Patanjali and many others because even today, the contributions of such great souls are found to be inspirational and relevant to the common people in any corner of India. Their examples serve the purpose of developing an inner strength so vital to human life. Savarkar and Hedgewar continued to implore not to ignore such perennial truths. Unfortunately, the last few decades were marked by unholy machinations of rejecting these truths.

Savarkar continued to proclaim the need to establish a Hindu *rashtra* by Hindufication of India at all costs. Though it could not happen during his lifetime, Narendra

Modi picked up the lost thread in 2013. Later, the Indian electorate stood firm and strong behind the pro-Hindutva stand of Modi and the BJP, first in the 2014 parliamentary elections followed by a bigger mandate in the 2019 elections. This decision-making power of the electorate was a clear message to the world that ultimately truth triumphs, not falsehood. Majority of the print media accepted the truth of the outcome of the 2019 election. The message is that India is a Hindu nation and once this fact is endorsed by the large majority, India can march ahead on the path of progress with indomitable courage. Voters experienced this spirit in the first five years of BJP rule and hence gifted even a bigger victory to the Narendra Modi-led BJP in 2019.

Swatantryaveer Savarkar pronounced these facts all his life and also predicted that supporters of this truth would be successful pilgrims of India. Much later has the Indian electorate accepted his words. Maulana Wahiduddin Khan had opined that the word 'Hindu' stands for and signifies the Indian way of life. Dr. APJ Abdul Kalam also endorsed this view. Syed Ata Hasnain does not say anything different. In fact, every mature and enlightened Muslim and Christian in India would support this balanced opinion. Savarkar was confident about this and that is why he appealed to all non-Hindus to come forward and march shoulder to shoulder on the path of making Hindu India happy and affluent. Savarkar had stated and is now a known fact that the fundamental nature of the Hindu community is marked by tolerance and inclusivity. That is why, in his autobiographial book, *Majhi Janmathep* (*My Life-imprisonment*), Savarkar stated that he had established a 'Hindu State' inside the Cellular Jail in Andaman in 1916 and it did not make any differentiation between Hindus and non-Hindus. The values worshipped in such a Hindu *rashtra* were natural justice and humanity.

Seniors' Views

Salman Khurshid and Abdul Gafoor Noorani

It was in July 2013 when Narendra Modi clarified in an interview that he was a strong supporter of the Hindu *rashtra*. The then Minister of External Affairs, Salman Khurshid vehemently attacked him. His criticism was that the very expression 'Hindu *rashtra*' has a contradiction in terms. 'Hindu,' he said, 'is a communal word and therefore making it signify a nation is completely wrong.' The same argument was advocated by Abdul Gafoor Noorani. When the so-called progressive intellectuals from the Hindu community also came out in support of this criticism, it was for S. Gurumurthy to write an article to blast this argument. We should understand his counter argument.

S. Gurumurthy

Swami Vivekananda, Yogi Arvind, Lal-Bal-Pal and Mahatma Gandhi, all of them have celebrated the contribution of the Hindu community in the development of India. The Supreme Court of India has given a verdict that the word 'Hindu' stands for the 'Indian way of life'. The Apex Court has endorsed the view of Maulana Wahiduddin Khan. Hence the word Hindu stands for the nation, not just for one community. 'Hindu' and '*rashtra*' are two words which go together; it is not a communal term.

'Khurshid says Modi's claim of being a Hindu nationalist is oxymoron. The dictionary meaning of 'oxymoron' is a speech in which opposite or contradictory ideas are combined, like 'thunderous silence' or 'sweet sorrow'. Similarly, according to Khurshid, 'Hindu and nationalism are opposites.' If the poor prose is excused, he may have only intended to say that religion and nationalism are contradictory. But is Hindu nationalism an oxymoron? Try this on those who had laid the foundation of Indian freedom in contemporary India.

Take Swami Vivekananda first. The Swami's nationalist exhortations deified the nation, sowing the seeds of the freedom movement. Vivekananda inspired the passivists as well as the revolutionaries. The tallest leaders, such as Mahatma Gandhi, Subhas Chandra Bose, Rajaji, Rabindranath Tagore and Jawaharlal Nehru, acclaim him. Even mystics like Maharishi Aurobindo and Subramanya Bharati were inspired by him. And what did Swami Vivekananda stand for? 'A nation in India,' declared Vivekananda, 'must be a union of those whose hearts beat in the same spiritual tune' (S. Gurumurthy, 'Aurobindo, Vivekananda and Gandhi too Oxymorons?', *Indian Express*, July 16th, 2013).

□

7

Loyalty to History

Thus Spoke Swatantryaveer Savarkar...

Hindu-Muslim Relations

In his preface to his book, *Hindu Padpadshahi*, Savarkar directly addressed the Muslim citizens. It is definitely worth studying. Said Savarkar:

'To our Muhammadan readers, however, a word of explanation is needed. The duty of a historian is primarily to depict as far as possible the feelings, motives, emotions and actions of the actors themselves, whose deed he aims to relate. This he cannot do faithfully and well, unless he, for the time being, rids himself not only of all prejudices and prepossessions, but even of the fears of the consequences the story of the past might be calculated to have on the interests of the present. That latter end he should try to serve by any other means than the falsification or exaggeration or underestimation of the intentions and actions of the past. A writer on the life of Muhammad, for example, would be wanting in his duty, if he tries to smoothen down the fierce attacks on "idolatry" and the dreadful threats held before the unbelievers by that heroic Arab, only to ingratiate himself with the sentiments of those of his fellow countrymen or readers who do not belong to the Moslem persuasion. He should try to do that by being himself more tolerant or even by drawing a moral more in consonance with reason and freedom of thought and worship... If he cannot do that, he had better give up the thought of writing the life of Muhammad altogether.'

History for the World Community

In the Preface to *Hindu Padpadshahi*, Savarkar has replied to the question, 'Why Read History?' The potently meaningful answer throws substantial light on the expected level of relationship between India and the Muslims:

'We ought to read history not with a view to find out the best excuse to perpetuate the old strife and stress, bickerings and bloodsheds, whether in the name of our blessed motherland, "of our Lord God", that divided man from man and race from race but precisely for the contrary reason of finding out the root causes that contributed to and the best means to the removal of that stress and strife, of those bickerings and bloodsheds, so that man may be drawn towards man because he is man, the child of our common father–God and nursed at the breast of our common Mother Earth and wield humanity into a World-Commonwealth.' (Author's Foreword to 'Hindu Padpadshahi', in *Selected Works of Veer Savarkar*, vol. 4, p. 10).

Conflict in the Present is Suicidal

'Especially our Muhammadan countrymen, against the deeds of whose ancestors the history under review was a joint it giants and mighty protest which we hold justifiable, will try to read it without attributing, solely on that ground that any ill feeling to us towards our Muhammadan countrymen of this generation or towards the community itself as such. It would be as suicidal and as ridiculous to borrow the hostilities and combats of the past only to fight them out into the present as it would be for Hindu and a Muhammadan to lock each other suddenly in a death grip while embracing, only because Shivaji and Afzal Khan had done so hundreds of years ago!" (ibid, pp. 9-10).

Current Situation and Analysis

Since 2014, pseudo-secularists in India are making it a point to launch a tirade against Veer Savarkar. They are using their tongues and their pens to vilify Savarkar without paying any heed to the do's and don'ts in the field of research. Against this background, it is vital to place on record how Savarkar himself was highly inclusive and balanced in his thoughts, expressions and conduct. Recalling this is an important need of the present.

India has adopted a plethora of new policies in the field of external affairs in the past. For example, when Pandit Jawaharlal Nehru was the Prime Minister, non-alignment was the fundamental characteristic of our foreign relations. The second important consideration was increasing friendship with Muslim countries. During the prime ministership of Indira Gandhi, we changed our direction from non-alignment to multiple alignments. In the post-Cold War period, we continued our friendly relations with the Muslim countries, but also started extending a hand of friendship to Israel. After Narendra Modi became the Prime Minister, the policy of multiple alignments and friendship with Israel became dominant and the speed of implementation increased multifold. We entered into bilateral agreements with several countries without feeling any compunctions. In this context also, it is pertinent to remember the Savarkar doctrine. Narendra Modi indeed took a quantum jump at a great speed in external affairs in the last six years. This was partly due to the fact that BJP had a clear majority in the Parliament, which gave it a free hand in shaping the new initiatives in external affairs. The present government can easily formulate and implement policies vis-a-vis other countries based on the sole criterion of protecting the national interests of India. Witnessing all this, we can certainly feel that the soul of Veer Savarkar would certainly be feeling gratified at these developments.

Accepting the Pragmatic

In the recent past, the Pakistan government placed the proposition of Kartarpur corridor. A number of experts contributed their thoughts. Their review may convince all that it is high time India adopted a distinctively robust and pragmatic policy in so far as dealing with China and Pakistan is concerned. That we need to leave behind dreamy and romantic strategies is imperative and agreed to by all experts. Had Savarkar spoken in soft and sweet terms, he too would have earned great popularity. However, for Savarkar, public good was more important than public praise. After several decades, the stance of Veer Savarkar preferring public welfare to public recognition is being accepted. In this connection, it should be appropriate to mention a sternly critical article by Brahma Chellaney, a well-known geo-strategist:

It was in November 2018 that Pakistan announced its intention to open the Kartarpur corridor. Not surprisingly, over-optimistic thinkers started flying kites of hope like "the corridor will encourage people's free traffic between India and Pakistan"..."disciples of Guru Nanak Dev will devoutly undertake pilgrimage from Suvarna Mandir in Amritsar to Kartarpur", etc. Even Narendra Modi expressed an optimistic view that just like 'the demolition of the Berlin wall paved the way for the unification of Germany,

Kartarpur corridor might unite India and Pakistan in the future!' However, Brahma Chellaney sang an entirely incoherent tune. He reminded his readers of a very striking and appalling incident in the history of India. King Prithviraj Chauhan displayed a noble soul when he allowed free access to a defeated and captive aggressor Mohammed Ghori. Indeed a generous gesture. It was his misfortune that when the tables turned, Mohammed Ghori took pleasure in brutally killing the defeated king Prithviraj Chauhan. He states that even after Independence and Partition, 'Indian rulers have copied Prithviraj Chauhan time and again, whereas Pakistani rulers have carried on the legacy of Mohammad Ghori.' In 1971, the Indian Army achieved glorious success in enfranchising Bangladesh and even capturing 93,000 Pakistani soldiers as prisoners-of-war. However, the then Prime Minister Indira Gandhi showed the same generous gesture as Prithviraj Chauhan and set these prisoners free unconditionally. Later on, Prime Minister Atal Behari Vajpayee also repeated a similar noble deed by travelling to Lahore by bus to extend a friendly hand to Pakistan. He also invited Parvez Musharraf to Agra, feeling that he was laying the foundation of a long-term friendship. The present Prime Minister invited the Pakistani Prime Minister for his own swearing-in ceremony. Modi also went to Pakistan to attend a family function of the Pakistani premier. Brahma Chellaney goes ahead to inform his readers that the generosity shown by Indiraji, Atalji and Narendraji has always been repaid by Pakistan in terms of virulent and atrocious conduct. In other words, we Indians seem not to learn our lessons from the past. That is why, a rogue enemy like Pakistan goes on becoming more and more of an unscrupulous rascal. As soon as Pakistan announced its plan to open the Kartarpur corridor, we

Indians felt so enamoured that we forgot the Pakistani attack in November 2018 on Mumbai and the martyrdom of head constable Tukaram Omble while capturing Ajmal Kasab. Setting aside this memory, we announced a policy to enhance friendship with Pakistan. But all that Pakistan was busy with was hatching a conspiracy to once again create a Khalistan in India. Brahma Chellaney has beautifully summed up his article by saying, 'All the leaders who have got into an ostrich-like habit of burying own nostrils in the sand and feeling that a sandstorm is not coming, leaders who become alert only at election time, should wake up and remember that a stitch in time saves nine!' (Brahma Chellaney, 'India's Kartarpour Headache', *Times of India*, December 14th, 2018, p. 14).

Swatantryaveer Savarkar had often done a clinical dissection of the typical Indian habit of overdoing virtue. He has even called it a 'virtuous perversion'! He wanted us to remain alert and vigilant and to imbibe appropriate lessons from our history. Our conduct with an enemy should always be governed by the tit-for-tat rule. The same vital principles of foreign policy have been displayed in the article by Brahma Chellaney. This leads to the conclusion that the Savarkar doctrine is evergreen and values espoused by him are immortal.

It is a matter of pleasure that the parliamentary standing committee on external affairs has also taken due notice of the anti-Indian machinations of China. It has recommended that 'India should, indeed loosen its self-imposed shackles in relation with China, especially on the three troublesome subjects—trade, Taiwan and Tibet'. It also suggests that we should not be extra sensitive or sentimental about China ('Don't be so Deferential' by Dilip Sinha, a formal diplomat, in *Times of India*, December 24th, 2018, p. 12).

□

8

"You are Our Own People!"

Thus Spoke Swatantryaveer Savarkar...

In his book, *Swatantryaveer Savarkar: A Mystery*, author D.N. Gokhale has narrated a very touching incident that happened during Savarkar's stay in Ratnagiri. It throws light on how affectionate Savarkar was with well-meaning Muslims.

It happened in 1928. A group of social workers from Ratnagiri was returning from Malvan by a boat, after completing a conference for the eradication of untouchability. They all sat together for lunch in the boat. The tiffin carried by Sawant Guruji had chicken, *puri* and some other snacks. Savarkar was comfortable with non-veg food. Some of them realised for the first time that Savarkar had no issues with eating non-vegetarian food. At the same time, the ticket inspector, Mr. Lala, a Muslim, approached them. Savarkar insisted that Lala should join the group for lunch. He made Lala bring his tiffin and shared his food along with others. He spoke to Lala affectionately. Later, Lala said, 'Tatyasaheb, we had a misconception that you hated Muslims. Today it has been cleared!' Savarkar laughed heartily and holding Lala's hand, exclaimed, 'Oh, come on! Are you some alien? You are our own people. If some Muslims hate us because we are Hindus, if some

Muslims desecrate temples and destroy idols, only they would be my enemies. Not all Muslims. I dislike bad deeds; not good people!'

Savarkar said about religion: 'Your food does not disturb any religion. Religion resides in the heart; not in one's stomach!'

Soon the boat reached the port of Ratnagiri. Lala ordered a launch to carry Savarkar and his luggage. He personally helped Savarkar to disembark and get into the launch. When the launch left, Savarkar and Lala were seen to be waving goodbye to each other in a very friendly manner (A.G. Salvi, *In the Company of Savarkar*, part 1, pp. 7-9).

Current Situation and Analysis

There is a genuine necessity to recall Savarkar's thoughts about non-Hindus and especially about Muslims. This is because at present, many self-proclaimed progressives and liberals are levelling wild and baseless accusations against Savarkar and Golwalkar Guruji. Strangely enough, after Donald Trump got elected as the President of the United States, it was being alleged that these two Indian leaders had emphatically propagated that only Hindus should be treated with respect in India and non-Hindus be relegated to secondary citizenship. This completely false charge was levelled simply because Narendra Modi happens to be a disciple of both Savarkar and Golwalkar. Modi's detractors analyse every speech and policy of his with a skewed vision for the same reason. An attack on the followers of Savarkar and Golwalkar is a direct attack on the the origins of pro-Hindutva thinking. Here is an example: 'Modi must surely be gratified by the militaristic diatribe as well as Trump's pledge to obliterate radical Islamic terrorism from the face of the earth' (*EPW* editorial, 'Two Nationalisms', January 28th, 2017, p. 9).

Truly speaking, trying to find and show any similarity between Donald Trump on the one hand and Savarkar-Golvalkar-Modi on the other is pure injustice to reality. Trump had taken several hard-hitting measures, such as banning the entry of citizens of seven Muslim States into the US and upholding discrimination between White Anglo-Saxon Protestant citizens and all others. He asked tough questions of several countries on how they would benefit the US. As against this, Savarkar, Golwalkar and their followers are simply advocating justice and humanity. In the definition of Hindutva as propagated by Swatantryaveer Savarkar, there are two important terms: *pitrubhu* (fatherland) and *punyabhu* (holy land). For all non-Hindus born in India, India is definitely the fatherland. All that Savarkar said was that if they also treated India as their holy land, we would accept them as nationalist non-Hindus. This message of Savarkar is extremely significant.

□

9

Who is a Hindu?

Thus Spoke Swatantryaveer Savarkar...

Prof. S.H. Deshpande has made a mention of an important extract from the book *Hindutva* written by Savarkar. It goes like this : 'any non-Hindu who accepts this land, the land of River Sindhu, as his 'holy land' (*punyabhu*), the land of his prophet and *rishi*, his God, devotee and *guru*, the land to which he owes his reverence and allegiance, and the land which contains his pious places of pilgrimage, is to be considered as a Hindu.'

Seniors' Views

1. Dr. D.N. Gokhale

Dr. D.N. Gokhale and Dr. P.L. Gawade are two eminent scholars who have studied the life, literature and work of Veer Savarkar. They both have given similar reviews on Savarkar's definition of Hindutva. In the preface of his book, *Hindutva Darshan*, Dr. Gokhale notes that non-Hindu citizens can be accepted as Hindus without changing their formal religion, if they accept India as their holy land.

2. Dr. P.L. Gawade

Dr. Gawade has written his well-researched Ph.D. thesis from which two important paragraphs run as follows:

'Savarkar's original definition of Hindutva was somewhat restrictive. However, after deeper thought, he adopted a wider political policy and expanded the horizons of his concept of Hindutva, so that it acquired a nationwide dimension. Evidence for this has been quoted by renowned author and journalist, Gajanan Tryambak Maadkholkar. In an article published in *Tarun Bharat* dated April 5th, 1962 and titled 'The Life-work of Dr. Hedgewar', he shows that Savarkar's notion on Hindutva expanded beyond the outward religious symptoms. Savarkar accepted that even after conversion to another religion, a person can still remain Hindu by culture.'

In this article, Maadkholkar has made a reference to a personal letter of Savarkar and has quoted the thinking of Devadatta Narayan Tilak as endorsed by Savarkar. It runs like this: 'Religious conversion does not mean cultural or social conversion. If a person abdicates Hinduism and embraces another religion, it does not mean that he has abdicated his culture and society. He can remain Hindu by culture even after the religious conversion. Two lines from a poem by Reverend Tilak, the father of Devdatta, who had embraced Christianity, are potent with meaning:

'ख्रिस्तयशोरत झालो तरी मी सोडी न जन्मधरेला
मरेन अपुल्या देशासाठी ख्रिस्ती जरी झालो'

This means, 'Though I have embraced the glory of Jesus Christ, there is no question of leaving the land of my birth. I will die for my country though I am now a Christian.'

3. Golwalkar Guruji

Golwalkar Guruji also accepted the stand of Veer Savarkar regarding the non-Hindus, especially the Muslims. The lines below are an excellent testimony of his stance: 'Our proposition is that Muslims and Christians should leave behind their feeling of alienation and should assimilate with the national mainstream of India.'

Guruji also asserted that 'several Muslims and Christians of India were converts from Hinduism either by force or due to misgivings and such other reasons. It is our duty to offer them a chance to return to their original home. They have missed their way. If we are able to bring them back, we will celebrate a great festival of lights. This is not by force or compulsion. This is a call out of love. This is a humble request. They should understand the turn of events and the reality and should come back to the fold of Hinduism, in terms of their attire, traditions and customs, domestic arrangements, way of conducting marriages and final rituals. They should assimilate with the original Hindu community. Some people claim that Hindus, Muslims and Christians, etc., are all one on the political and economic levels of existence. However, why should this unity be limited only to these levels? Why should it not be introduced on a wider and more inclusive level? Why should we not appeal to our estranged brothers and sisters to come back and get accommodated within our society, coexist with great love within the Hindu way of life and Hindu religion? To those who speak about unity on political and economic fronts, we would like to respond that we expect not only political and economic, but also cultural and religious unification.'

4. Prof. S.H. Deshpande

Prof. Deshpande has made a very pertinent comment on this extract of Golwalkar Guruji. He says that a proper study of this extract will show that Guruji appeals to Muslims and Christians to return to Hindu religion. However, his appeal comes out of love, not out of force. Additionally, when he mentions Hindu religion, what he really implies is Hindu culture because he is willing to offer them the freedom of worshipping Allah or Christ. Guruji even says that Hindus can celebrate Eid!

5. Rajiv Sane

Mr. Sane regularly contributes thoughtful articles to daily *Loksatta* and other periodicals. In an article titled 'Why Do the Materialists Accept Hindutva?' he criticises leaders of the Congress and liberal progressive parties for their anti-Hindu politics that is based largely on a silly equation that precaution related to Islam is equal to hatred for Muslims! (*Loksatta*, November 7th, 2018) In another article, Rajiv Sane states that in the pre-Independence years, the Hindus were a continuously beaten and vulnerable community. It was a poignant need to understand the feelings and emotions of this community, with due empathy. The pro-Hindutva thinking of Savarkar fulfilled this need. On the other hand, the liberal progressive groups stamped as an unacceptable person (*persona non grata*) anyone who was even remotely concerned with Hindutva (*Loksatta*, December 26th, 2018). To sum up, it is an extremely precious standpoint that we should try to understand the Savarkar doctrine afresh in the contemporary situation.

□

10

Hindu Philosophy

Thus Spoke Swatantryaveer Savarkar...

In order to understand Savarkar's attitude towards non-Hindus, we should study his appeal to them, especially to the Muslims:

'Hindu philosophy has established all the feasible conjectures about the nature of the unknown and about the relationship between the eternal and the temporal. You may believe in a single God or in multiple deities, you may be an atheist or an agnostic, whoever you are, hey *atman*, this temple offers you ample scope for offering love, completing the process of self-development and achieving ultimate satisfaction. This is so because this temple does not stand on the strength of any single personality but on the strong foundation of Truth...'

Current Situation and Analysis

At present Prime Minister Narendra Modi does not discriminate among citizens on the basis of caste, creed or religion. All that he expects is that Muslims should not expect the power of veto. As noted earlier, he dropped the name of Aurangzeb from Aurangzeb Marg in New Delhi, but it is more pertinent to note that the road has now been named after Dr. APJ Abdul Kalam. This clearly tells us that today's India respects and revers Muslims like Dr. Kalam. If you glance at the foreign policy of Donald Trump, it centres unilaterally around American interests whereas the external affairs policy of Modi government thinks it important to show leniency to neighbours, like Bangladesh. It is an open truth that all the Muslim countries, ranging from the Mediterranean to the Persian Gulf, have been treated in a very just and fair manner by the Modi government. These countries have also realised that the Modi government is practising genuine secularism in India. There is no doubt that the present Indian rulers are implementing balanced and inclusive policies with respect to the non-Hindus as was preached by Savarkar and Golwalkar.

The Indian electorate has also been convinced that just as Rahul Gandhi's secularism is synthetic and untrue, his nationalism also is equally a false façade. The Congress loves only the votes. Its love for the Muslims prior to 2014 and its newly found infatuation for the Hindu voters' feelings post-2014, both signify high drama.

Indians are now asking difficult questions of Congress leaders when they pay visits to *mutths* and temples. Will the Congress promise to really care for the Hindus in India henceforth? Will the trio of Sonia, Rahul and Priyanka willingly acknowledge that Jawaharlal Nehru's opposition to the resurrection of the Somnath temple in Saurashtra was a mistake and is not acceptable to the Congress today? The opposition of the Congress to construct Ram Mandir in Ayodhya has always offended the Hindu sentiments. Can they acknowledge it as a grave error? Will they recognise the fact that Sardar Vallabhbhai Patel, Rajarshi Tandon and Lal Bahadur Shastri, despite being Congress leaders, loved Hinduism? The right way ahead for the Congress is to support the construction of the Ram temple and to acknowledge that many non-Hindus in India are also disciples of the Indian culture. Henceforth, they should be taken with us to present real cultural nationalism of India to the world.

Soft Hindutva of Congress

The world has realised the changing mindset of the Indian electorate due to the parliamentary elections of 2014. It was then that everybody took notice of the fact that the Indian citizens felt devoted to Hindu religion and Hindu culture and cared for their emotional universe. It was as a fallout of this change that the Congress thought of changing its strategy and pleasing its Hindu voters by showing some concern, at least outwardlly, for the emotional well-being of the Hindus. The Congress headquarters decided that things that they despised upto 2014 should now be held as respectable. It was then that leaders, right from Rahul Gandhi, changed their working style and their direction of election campaigning. Some 18 years ago, Narendra Modi for Congress was the dealer in deaths and the avowed enemy of Muslims. But this epithet of Narendra Modi has vanished from the Congress propaganda in the last few years.

Experts' Views

1. Prof. Mohammed Ayuub

Prof. Mohammed Ayuub, working as a researcher in the think-tank 'Centre for Global Policy' in Washington DC, USA has written an analytical article in *The Hindu* of May 24th about the changing working style of the Congress. He writes, 'While running the election campaign for 2019 parliamentary polls, the Congress neither underlined the secularist values, nor did it uphold minoritarianism, nor did it put forth how Muslims were neglected. All the efforts of Rahul Gandhi and his accomplices were aimed at communicating to the electorate that they were not a party interested in appeasement of Muslims. Going further, Rahul Gandhi took the lead to demonstrate his reverence for the Hindu sentiments. That is how the "soft Hindutva" of the Congress was born! What followed was Rahul being vigorously presented as a *janeuu*-wearing Brahmin, visiting one temple today and the other tomorrow. Rahul was under the impression that the Indian voters would approve and put their stamp on the soft Hindutva of the Congress, driving away the extreme and hard Hindutva of Narendra Modi. Rahul forgot that the Indian voter was capable of distinguishing between the genuine and artificial. It rejected the spurious version of Hindutva. Willy-nilly Congress acknowledged that Indian nationalism and Hindu nationalism are two sides of the same coin.'

Mr. Mohammed Ayuub specially mentions Hindu nationalism. In other words, he is telling his readers that ultimately the Congress also tried to subscribe to the Savarkar school of thought.

It is noteworthy, though not amusing, as to what kind of somersaults the Congress has taken in the last 90 years. Jawaharlal Nehru had to succumb to the pressure of staunch Muslims when he took lead in the Khilafat movement. Now his great grandson, keen on wooing the Hindu electorate, has performed a somersault! In spite of this, as elections drew closer, Rahul realised that voters from Amethi were not likely to accept his duplicate version of Hindutva and that Smriti Irani might defeat him in the election. Apprehension of a defeat prompted the decision to contest from a second constituency, that is, Wayanad in Kerala, because it was dominated by Muslim voters. The election results proved his fear to be true. Smriti Irani indeed trounced Rahul in his one-time fortress of Amethi constituency. This is because the mature voters had by now understood that they should opt for the genuine version rather than an artificial one.

2. Ravi Shankar Prasad

Union Cabinet Minister for Telecommunications Mr. Ravi Shankar Prasad recently gave a speech at a function in Delhi, where he rightly pointed out, 'Today BJP is in power in 15 states, in addition to its single-party majority government at the Centre. In spite of this, have we done any injustice or harm to any Muslim? On the contrary, we would like to respect such Muslims who value and help the common citizens of the country. At Jalpaiguri in West Bengal, Anwar-ul-Haq has been helping needy patients for the last several years by taking them to the hospital on his bike. After realising this, Prime Minister Narendrabhai himself called this social worker on phone and informed him of the decision to award him the Padma Shri. Anwar-ul-Haq is a worker in a tea garden. We deem it our duty to honour such respectable gentlemen' (*Indian Express*, Mumbai, April 22nd, 2017, pp. 3-4).

□

11

An Appeal to Muslims

Thus Spoke Swatantryaveer Savarkar...

'Why go then to fill your little pitcher to wells far off, when you stand on the banks of the crystal-streamed Ganges herself? Does not the blood in your veins, O brother of our common forefathers, cry aloud with the recollections of the dear old scenes and ties from which they were so cruelly snatched away at the point of the sword? Then come back to the fold of your brothers and sisters who with arms extended are standing at the open gate to welcome you–their long-lost kith and kin. You, who by race, by blood, by culture, by nationality possess almost all the essentials of Hindutva and had been forcibly snatched out of our ancestral home by the hand of violence–you have only to render wholehearted love to our common mother and recognise her not only as fatherland (*pitrubhu*), but even as a holyland (*punyabhu*) and you would be most welcome to the Hindu–fold. This is a choice which our countrymen and our old kith and kin, the Bohras, Khojas, Memons and other Mohammedan and Christian communities are free to make–a choice again which must be a choice of love (V.D. Savarkar, *Hindutva*, pp. 144-146).

Saying 'No' to Veto

The presidential speech delivered by Savarkar at the Nagpur session of Hindu Mahasabha shines due to its amazing clarity:

'It would be simply preposterous to endow the Moslem minority with the right of exercising a practical veto on the legitimate rights and privileges of the majority and call it a *swarajya*. The Hindus do not want a change of masters; they are not going to struggle and fight and die only to replace an Edward by an Aurangzeb simply because the latter happens to be born within Indian borders, but they want henceforth to be masters themselves in their own house, in their own land'(*Selected Works of Veer Savarkar*, vol. 4, 2007, p. 289).

Appropriate Answer

The Sindh Muslim League held its conference in October 1938 at Karachi, Sindh. Its leader Fazlul Haque told the audience, 'If an eight-year old boy, Muhammad bin-Qasim, could win the Sindh province with the help of only 18 soldiers, eight crore Muslims can definitely win the entire India.' His listeners heartily clapped and responded by saying, 'Just give us an order and we will die to execute it.'

The samc Fazlul Haque boasted again and Swatantryaveer Savarkar gave him a befitting reply. This exchange of words is also worth mentioning. While Haque said, 'The Muslims are tigers and lions and they will harass the Hindus', Veer Savarkar replied, 'The history of creation proves that it is men who have reclaimed the earth and lions and tigers had to retire to the obscurity of the forest. We Hindus are men. One man with a whip in his hand controls scores of lions and tigers in a circus and these beasts obey wonderfully well.' (Dr. P.L. Gawade, *Savarkar: Ek Chikitsak Abhyas*, p. 276).

Current Situation and Analysis

It was Savarkar who aroused courage and valour in the Hindu community in the pre-partition period. It was he who nourished the spirit of self-respect and quest for triumph among the Hindus. And it was he who dared to exchange hot words to counter the insolent bragging of the Muslims. As a result, Hindus in Punjab, Bengal and Bihar could show some tough and straight spine to resist the aggressive behaviour of Muslim extremists. The Muslim League was insisting on a safe corridor tearing through the breadth of India to serve as a Pak-owned road link between West Pakistan and East Pakistan. It was only due to the courage and bravery shown by some protesting Hindus, inspired by the messages of Savarkar, that this vile ambition of Muslim League bit dust. That is why Dr. Syama Prasad Mookherjee could say with a gratified heart, 'We partitioned the partition.'

The conclusion is that we Hindus should never nurse any guilt about the blunt and outspoken speeches of Veer Savarkar. On the contrary, we should be ever grateful to this great man for his indomitable spirit. It is because Hindus do not hate the religious thoughts of others or discriminate. Differences of opinion are welcomed, but at the same time, the Hindus do not compromise with vital values, such as their core identity. In times of need, the Hindus can display anger and be disruptive, but at heart, they are basically inclusive and forgiving because they know that they have to walk ahead by taking along all those who stay in India and therefore the awareness that all are Indians should always light like a lamp. It is important to remember that the Savarkar doctrine is a finely balanced and coordinated equation of the spirit of tolerance and the spirit of conquest!

International Politics

We have already clarified in the previous pages how significant changes which have taken place in internal politicking and governance since 2014 are coherent with the Savarkar school of thinking. Indian nationalism is neither regional nor territorial; it is cultural in nature. That is why internal politics under prime ministership of Narendra Modi has remained complementary and supplementary to the culture and civilisation of India. Our conclusion so far is that Prime Minister Narendra Modi is giving shape to the dreams of Savarkar.

Since 1930, aggressiveness and bullying tactics of the Muslims had been increasing at break-neck speed, while the Hindu community was leading a life of helplessness, inaction and lack of unity. On top of all this, the Congress, the socialist and communist parties were continuously administering to Hindus doses in tution of tolerance, forgiveness and indulgence. On the other hand, leaders of the Muslim League were brazenly instigating ordinary Muslims to resort to arms. Even today, our pseudo-secularists blame Savarkar for what actually was a very just and fair stand and prefer to remain tongue-tied on the fire-spewing speeches made by leaders of the Muslim League, particularly around 1938. It is important to explain their double standards and discriminating tendency to today's generation.

Senior's Views

M.P. Rege

The *Navbharat* magazine published from Wai (district Satara in Maharashtra) came out with a special issue devoted to the centenary of Congress, in February 1986.

They published in it a very logical article titled 'Politics of Indian Muslims' written by well-known philosopher, Meghashyam Pundalik Rege. This article exposed the typical Muslim mindset in the pre-Independence years. Here is an extract:

'From the point of view of Muslim leaders, the struggle for Indian Independence was a struggle by the Hindus to wrestle political power from the British. In this dispute, the interests of the Muslim and the British were common and hence they were natural partners. According to the views of Muslim leaders, the Indian political movement at that time contained another movement. It was by the Muslims against the Hindus. The Muslims solicited a lion's share of whatever political power would be transferred by the British to the Indians. This share had to be disproportionate to the Muslim population. For obtaining such a much higher share, the Muslims needed the support of the British. So the strategy of the Muslims was two-pronged. On the one hand, try to usurp the best possible share of power, on the other, always stay on the right side of the British power, to ensure that the Muslim community benefits' (*Navbharat* magazine, Congress Centenary special issue, pp. 161-162).

□

12

Armament Preparedness

Thus Spoke Swatantryaveer Savarkar...

As early as 1954, Swatantryaveer Savarkar had said: 'We should have started our efforts to empower our armed forces with modern equipment and should have expanded and well equipped our infantry, navy and airforce. We should have started doing all this right from the day on which this magnificent Indian Republic was established. Unfortunately, however, we have wasted the last six years. We have spent this time in inaugurating anything trivial from Neera distribution centres to afforestation campaigns, which were really secondary. Such things also have some utility, but it is like that of toys for young children. When you have a huge State to run and when you are aware that it has been surrounded by enemies, you should decide that your first priority is to enhance our readiness to protect the republic in all strategic fronts and manners. But we have neglected this most important duty as if we were determined to overlook it' (*Savarkar Vichar Darshan*, vol. 8, p. 265).

Current Situation and Analysis

The matter that follows is aimed at reviewing the international political strategies of the Modi government and to prove with due evidence that the current trend of international relations from India's strategic angle underlines the practical outlook of Savarkar's school of thinking. We celebrated the 51st death anniversary of Veer Savarkar in 2017. On which background was it celebrated? And in the current political scenario in the world, how is it that the foreign policies of Modi government follow the thought currents of the Savarkar doctrine?

At present, various thinkers are proposing that India should cast away its inferiority complex and march ahead in international politics with greater confidence. Prime Minister Narendra Modi is also showing amazing skill and acumen in enhancing the Indian influence in the global scenario. Thus the situation also is encouraging India and the Indian leadership is in a position to milk the situation for the greater good of its foreign affairs policy. Even a cursory review of this cycle of events will be able to underline the fact that the expectations of Veer Savarkar are almost automatically getting fulfilled.

Savarkar had expressed his deep anguish in 1954 when he said that we were falling behind the world in armament preparation and in acquisition of contemporary arms and ammunition. But in 2014, i.e. after 60 years' lapse, our country started taking steps in the direction of harnessing science and technology for empowering the defence forces of the country. This put an end to the hesitations of the last 60 years. Around the 50th death anniversary of Savarkar, we in fact took a very significant leap. On September 24th, 2014, ISRO (Indian Space Research Organisation) achieved a colossal success by placing India's 'Mangalyaan' in the sphere of gravity of the Mars. It was a global record because no other country had accomplished such a task in such a limited period of preparation and within such a restricted budget. Looked at from this point of view, it is clear that we have left behind China in space technology. Later, in June 2016, we were successful in attempting a fusion of Sukhoi 30 fighter planes and Brahmos missiles. We were able to install our supersonic missiles, Brahmos, in Sukhoi 30. This was a joint development project of two friendly countries–India and Russia. Brahmaputra is the largest Indian river while Mosqua is a similar Russian river. Brahmos, the name, is a fusion of these two great rivers! Its combination with Sukhoi 30 has doubled the striking capacity of the Indian Airforce. Sukhoi 30 can fly for 3000 kms in one go. Brahmos installed on to it is able to hit a target 3300 kms away. Only a limited number of countries have such a capacity for firing missiles from space, thereby also enhancing their own security. India now is one of them.

By a stroke of good luck, during the visit of Narendra Modi to the US in June 2016, India was included in the missile technology regulating system and received the green signal to erect six atomic reactors proposed by India. This way the Modi government could reduce India's loneliness in the field of atomic energy. Of course it is a bitter fact that India has not yet succeeded in getting the membership of the nuclear suppliers' group, but then again, on December 26th, 2016, India successfully conducted the Agni 5 intercontinental ballistic missile test and proved to the world that its striking capacity has increased to the range of 5,000 kms. This way, India has clearly proved to the world that it has the capacity of preventing China from any misconceived adventure. The table given below is enough to show how India has been enhancing its resistance ability continuously:

Agni 1	:	700 kms
Agni 2	:	2000 kms
Agni 3 & 4	:	2500 to 3500 kms
Agni 5	:	5000 kms

As expected, the Chinese mass media have bombarded India with severe criticism and so has Pakistan. No wonder India neglected the unfriendly duo's reactions, because the entire world is aware of the image of India as a responsible and peace-loving nation. The successful testing of Agni 5 has not done any damage to this image.

In 2017, ISRO fire-launched 104 satellites at a time into the orbit, breaking the past records. Before this, Russia had launched 37 satellites in one go. India did it with 104 satellites, almost triple the number! Some four decades ago, India was very much a laggard in this field. But in the 21st century, we have come to the forefront in space technology. In May 2017, India launched the South Asia satellite as a gift to its neighbours. The original idea was to help all the SAARC countries to achieve progress in communication technology, but Pakistan declined to participate. Other countries in South Asia joined hands to take advantage of this satellite. Now none can say that India had omitted Pakistan. The onus is on Pak for isolating itself due to its stubborn attitude.

Savarkar: A Visionary

Veer Savarkar had written an essay titled 'Two Cultures in Two Words' which later became very famous. He has recommended therein that instead of the word '*shruti-smriti puranokta*', which means 'as told by the old scriptures', we should use the word 'up-to-date'. India, after 2014, has really progressed towards adopting all that is up-to-date, modern and contemporary. That makes Savarkar and his suggestion highly relevant today.

All the dreams of Savarkar are now getting fulfilled in the present! There are several proofs in his writing that he was a great visionary and that he could correctly judge the future turn of events. The Soviet Union disintegrated in 1991. It had vowed to bury capitalism but could not survive very long itself. After that, within a decade, the twin towers of the World Trade Centre in New York were devastated in an Islamic terrorist attack. This posed a threat to the US and to the capitalism so dear to its heart. This can also be interpreted in another manner. One can conclude that the sunset of the Euro-Atlantic world is sending shivers down the spine of the white people. A night gets over and a new day dawns. Just like this natural cycle, the Euro-Atlantic universe is gradually fading into oblivion and is giving way to the rise of the Indo-Pacific world. In other words, the Indian Ocean and the Pacific Ocean are becoming more dominant by replacing the hegemony of the Atlantic. From our point of view, an important development is the rise of greater South Asia and destiny's indications that India should be the leader in the emergence of a greater South Asia. On the other side, the menace of Islamic terrorism is growing in size and its heat is blasting the Euro-Americans as well as Muslims too. All those who are suffering have great expectations from India. How should India deal with them? Is the age old policy of non-alignment still relevant? Or does it need modification in line with the changing times? Adequate contemplation had already been done by the visionary Savarkar and it can help resolve many of these issues. To sum up, evidence of the far-reaching vision of Veer Savarkar can be perceived in matters such as the sunset on the Euro-Atlantic period and sunrise of Indo-Pacific period; the emergence of a greater South Asia with India leading it; the unchecked spread of Islamic terrorism, countries and societies victimised due to it and their expectations from India, and changes in India's foreign policy. More explanation of these follows in Section 14.

Seniors' Views

Why India is still not a Super Power

1. Bharat Karnad

If we list the names of thinkers who have recommended that 'India should move forward with greater confidence and take a leap in the global arena,' the first name should be that of Bharat Karnad. His book bearing the title, 'Why India is Not a Great Power Yet?' is the talk of the town. He says, 'India has a colossal landmass, huge quantum of natural resources, strength of well-educated youth and legacy of precious ancient culture. But we seem to have failed in exploiting these favourable circumstances to our advantage.' Karnad has not only exposed the issue but also pointed out that 'we have embraced some wrong and outdated notions. We have surrendered to a misgiving that if we are gentle and well-behaved, no country in the world will attack us! After Independence, the United States and the Soviet Union, both had offered us membership of the Security Council of the United Nations. But we declined it and we also rejected their suggestion to become equipped with atomic weapons. In conclusion, we lost historic opportunities of marching forward with gusto and of creating an impression on the world.' Having contributed these precious gems, Bharat Karnad comes to the favourable situation in the present times and appreciates Narendra Modi for understanding the situation and undertaking to build a global strategy without any compunctions. Sachin Diwan, in his review of Karnad's book says in the newspaper Loksatta of January 9th, 2016: 'India should now expand its sphere of influence; India should set its eyes much beyond the Persian Gulf, Gulf of Aden and straits of Malacca. In order to protect its interest and check the undue influence of China, India should take steps, such as connecting the Chabahar port in Iran to Central Asia by developing the Zaranj- Delaram Highway, expanding the movement of its Navy upto Simon's Town naval base near Cape Town in South Africa, enhance the existence of Indian armed forces in strategic locations, such as Furkhor air base in Tajikistan, Agalega Island in Mauritius and the naval base of En Trang in Vietnam, resuming nuclear testing which was suspended after Pokhran-2, becoming an atomic power as early as possible, setting up atomic armament in the direction of China, increasing the speed of economic and military reforms, taking a stronger position in world politics, including a tit-for-tat policy and not hesitate if it becomes necessary to use military power.' To conclude, this book expresses the dire need of India to leave behind its soft-State image and spread its wings on the global horizon. Karnad has scored out the popular misconception that a poor country like India should not place much emphasis on enhancing its military power. He has insisted that a determined forward march towards becoming a Super Power should continue while we grapple with internal issues. He underlines the need for adopting the mindset of a Super Power for initiating and succeeding in all these strategic actions.

2. Maharaj Krishna Rasgotra

Maharaj Krishna Rasgotra, a veteran thinker-diplomat with rich experience in foreign affairs, has written a book, *A Life in Diplomacy*. It corroborates the standpoint of Bharat Karnad. Rasagotra has criticised the foreign policy of Jawaharlal Nehru. John F. Kennedy, the then American President was of the opinion that India should develop

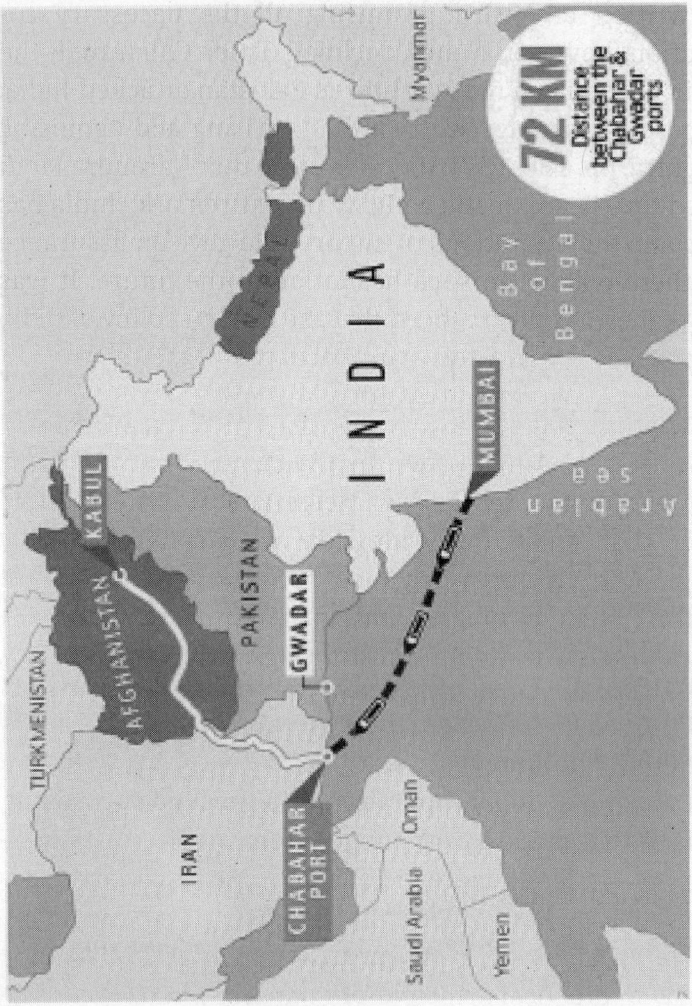

West Coast of India

atomic weapons because he thought that being a major democratic Asian country, India was the fittest in the Asian region for possessing nuclear weaponry. Kennedy had written to Nehru promising all the necessary co-operation, however, Nehru declined. Later China took the lead in becoming a nuclear power. Pakistan attacked India. All these happenings were both surprising and agonising (Rasgotra, pp. 186-187). It was in 2016 that Narendra Modi toured the US and made a highly potent remark, 'India has overcome the hesitations of history!' He gave an assurance that there will be no such hesitation in the future. It was then that everybody realised that the foreign policy of India had taken a new and decisive direction.

3. Nirupama Rao

As India's Ambassador to China and the US before being elevated as the Foreign Secretary of India, she had opined that 'under the leadership of Narendra Modi, the foreign policy of India has been developing a triumphant mindset.' Her statement that 'firm actions are getting reflected in the contemporary foreign policy of India,' is quite self-explanatory (*The Hindu*, March 4th, 2016, p. 11).

4. Brahma Chellaney

Enjoying a global reputation as a great geo-strategist, Chellaney has made a very pungent remark that 'during the tenure of Mr. Modi, meretricious doctrines are very rarely observed' (*The Hindu*, December 4th, 2014, p. 10).

Meretricious doctrines mean apparently attractive but actually impractical principles. In the light of this remark, it will be easy to understand how the foreign policy of India has taken some pragmatic turns since 2014.

5. Rajiv Sikri

Since he was India's Ambassador to Kazakhstan, his evaluation is worth mentioning: 'Narendra Modi does not approach the world in the role of a weak beggar. He travels the world with great confidence and with such vision that India should emerge as a major global power centre ('Redefining Governance', editor Anirban Ganguly, p. 130).

The Modi government has taken steps to make India uptodate, capable of self-defence and dominant in diplomacy. It is clear from the remarks of these learned experts and diplomats that Modi and the concerned ministers along with top officers of the External Affairs Ministry have implemented effective campaigns in this direction. Looking at their achievements, one can arrive at the conclusion that the expectations expressed by Veer Savarkar in 1954 from the Government of India are actually being brought to reality by the current dispensation.

6. Sameer Karve

An expert in warfare strategy, Karve throws light on this flight of India: 'Our Brahmos missile is now well-equipped to hit targets from naval warships into air, from a submarine into the air, and from air to land through Sukhoi 30. Now onwards when we get the fifth-generation advanced fighter planes like Rafael, they can also be ready for installation of Brahmos. If India can become a member of the missile-technology control regime, we will be able to export this technology easily to other countries' (*Maharashtra Times*, July 3rd, 2016).

Ultramodern, Scientific and Indigenous

The three holy words that Swatantryaveer Savarkar chanted all his life were 'ultra modern, scientific and indigenously produced'. It was always dear to his heart that his country should progress in the light of these three precious concepts and that the Indian citizens should not waste time on some naive, glittery and dreamy world, but be always awake, alert and active in a robust, real and rock-solid world which is good for their nation. Against this background, we can observe that today our Army, Navy and Airforce are taking strides towards becoming ultra modern. We are now getting prepared to arrest the probable missile attacks by our enemy, which can otherwise destroy the strategically important destinations and major cities in the country. As a preventive measure, our armed forces are getting equipped with indigenously produced anti-missile security systems. We have already decided to import S300 and S400 anti-missile systems from Russia. But more importantly, we have chosen to make them in India in the near future. These systems include radars which can identify enemy war planes and missiles even 800 kms away. Our intention is to increase their range from 800 kms to 1500 kms. Sachin Diwan has made available some more important information in this regard: 'On this path, we have included AEWACS (airborne early warning and control systems) which will enhance the anti-missile acting capacity of our armed forces. Separate systems will be installed exo-atmosphere and endo-atmosphere. Prithvi air defence missile will be useful for hitting down enemy missiles which are far away' ('The Story of Weaponry', *Loksatta*, December 22nd, 2018, p. 4).

Dr. A.S. Pillai, recipient of Padma Bhushan and father of Brahmos missiles developed indigenous technology to instal these missiles on Sukhoi 30MKI aeroplanes. As a result, we save our precious foreign exchange and from 250 million US dollars the contract came crashing down to 2.7 million US dollars. Russia thought it fit to accept this contract' ('Made in India' by Bhavesh Brahmankar, *Maharashtra Times*, December 10th, 2018, p. 9).

We have recently added two categories of heavy mortar guns: Howitzer and Vajra to our armaments. It has also been announced that ISRO (Indian Space Research Organisation) will send three Indian astronauts in space in 2022. This means that our dream to enter space will be fulfilled at the time of the platinum jubilee of Indian Independence!

This is how the insistence of Veer Savarkar on ultra modernism, on scientific attitude and on top priority to indigenous production is getting fulfilled.

□

13

What's Eternal?

Thus Spoke Swatantryaveer Savarkar...

In the year 1902, when Veer Savarkar was just 20-years old, he wrote a poem titled 'What's Permanent in this World?' This Marathi poem was published by two periodicals *Aryan Weekly* and *Kaal*. In the five stanzas of this poem, Savarkar states that the Persian empire, which had once trounced the eastern kingdoms, ultimately bit the dust. The valiant Greek warriors, under the leadership of Alexander, overpowered the Persian empire. After some time, the Roman empire became so mighty that it put an end to the Greek empire! The last two stanzas of the poem take a leap into a perpetually true theory. They lead to an assurance that the readers can keep their faith alive: even now it will be possible for the Easterners to overcome the Western powers. The last two stanzas are reproduced below:

हा उन्नती अवनतीस समुद्र जातो।
भास्वान् रवीही उदयास्त अखंड घेतो।
उत्कर्ष आणि अपकर्ष समान ठेले।
विश्वात आजवरि शाश्वत काय झाले?
जे मत्त फारचि बलान्वित गर्ववाही।
उद्विग्न-मानस उदासहि जे तयांही।
हे पाहिजे स्वमनि संतत चिंतियेले।

विश्वात आजवरि शाश्वत काय झाले ?

[The ocean continuously goes through tide and ebb. The day-maker, the Sun, himself rises and sets without fail every day. This proves that prosperity and downfall are equal and cyclical. So what's eternal in this world?

The mighty who feel proud and insolent and others who often feel distressed and gloomy, all should always keep this in their minds: What's eternal in this world?]

Current Situation and Analysis

Before writing this poem at the age of 20, Savarkar had taken an oath at the feet of Goddess Ashtabhuja at the tender age of 16 that he would walk the path treaded by revolutionaries and martyrs like the Chapekar brothers. True to his oath, he spent the rest of his life in following his oath rigorously. This brave person, who asked a very pertinent question as to which empire has lasted forever in this world, fought fearlessly against the mighty British Empire. During the eight years following 1902, his actions shook the British Empire as never before. Savarkar himself wrote a letter, entirely in poetic form, to Yesu Vahini, his elder brother's wife, summarising his group's achievements. Here is a couplet that oozes deep confidence:

नाही पुरी उलटली जरि आठ वर्षे।
तो कार्यसिद्धी इतुकी मन का न हर्षे।
आसेतुपर्वत उचंबळला प्रदेश।
वीराकृती धरित टाकुनी दीन वेष।।

[Not even eight years have passed since we started working, but the achievements are so many that they please our minds. We have shaken the land from the ocean to the Himalaya. We have thrown off the gloomy attires and have taken up a warrior's aptitude!]

During this period of eight years, from 1902 to

1910, India witnessed the beginning of the co-operative movement. It also saw the *swadeshi* movement (favouring boycott of British goods and use of only indigenously produced goods and materials). It was in this period that Viceroy Lord Curzon announced the Partition of the state of Bengal. This unjust decision ignited the fire of unrest all over India. Most importantly, this period saw the beginning of the bomb era in the Indian struggle for Independence. Khudiram Bose, a revolutionary, experimented with a bomb to assassinate Kings Ford, a British officer. Anant Kanhere killed the British Collector Jackson at Nasik in Maharashtra and Madan Lal Dhingra shot dead Curzon Wiley. During these eight years, Veer Savarkar himself created a network of revolutionaries in India. He then went to London, the capital of the British Empire, and celebrated the anniversary of the first armed struggle for Indian Independence that took place in 1857. In his book about martyrs and martyrdom, V.S. Joshi informs that in the decade prior to 1911, not a week went by without any major uprising in India against British rule. It was during this decade that great leaders like Lokmanya Tilak and Maharshi Aurobindo were subjected to long-term imprisonments. To conclude, Veer Savarkar at his young age, declared resolutely that the British empire was not there with a licence to immortality. And he almost immediately started working vigorously and more resolutely to blast the very foundations of the British Empire, not just from India, but even from London.

Real *Karmayog*

Both Savarkar and Dr. Hedgewar were visionary leaders who advocated similar standpoints, viz. 'the Hindu citizens of India should come together as Hindus. We should bury our small-time differences, outdated traditions and petty disagreements. We should unite in order to immortalise the eternal and precious values which have been handed down to us. We should come together from an emotional and constructive viewpoint. Our day-to-day lives should clearly reflect Hindu values of life. These life values are so attractive that even non-Hindus will be enamoured by them, just as black bees get attracted naturally to flowers because of their fragrance. The principle of gravity presupposes the gravitational pull, due to the greatness of the puller. Hindus should be the pullers without any prejudice or malice towards anyone. Our first priority is to develop the united strength of the Hindus. We should do it from an emotional point of view throughout the country and throughout our life-time. This is like spiritual *sadhana* which achieves fulfilment only if it does not presume and preclude any ambition for personal success or reputation. Both Savarkar and Hedgewar continued to strive relentlessly. They brought into practice the real *karmayog*. The Indians reaped the fruit of the duo's labour much later, in the results of the parliamentary elections of 2014 and 2019.

Senior's Views

Shrinivas Dikshit

The progress and development that happened in the five years post-2014 under the leadership of Narendra Modi, were along the lines of the Savarkar doctrine. That is why voters re-elected the BJP candidates with large margins. Shrinivas Dikshit, thinker from Maharashtra, had written an article '*Hindu Rashtrawad*' in 1980. He had predicted: 'There is a felt need that Hindu nationalists should propagate a way of life, based on the eternal values of the Hindus. Just as meteors floating in the space get attracted towards the earth because of its gravitational pull, non-Hindu communities in India should be attracted towards Hindutva, due to the beauty of the Hindu way of life. They should come by attraction, not by coercion. The Hindu society and the movement presently do not have that magnanimous gravitation. Naturally, how could attraction happen in the absence of such magnanimous gravity? We should change our way of life with reference to the eternal values. There is also a felt need to further liberalise the values and make them more noble. Hindu nationalism should not thrive on the hatred for Muslims or any other community. Our well-known national ideal is that we bear friendship in our minds towards all the living beings and malice towards none (Shrinivas Dikshit, '*Hindu Rashtrawad*', *Navbharat* magazine, April 1980, pp. 25-38).

□

14

Political Pendulum Swings to the East

Thus Spoke Swatantryaveer Savarkar...

In the year 1902, Savarkar, as an adventurous youth, had predicted that 'those Eastern countries which have now been colonised, will emerge victorious in the future and the Western emperors, who have illegally occupied them as colonies, will go into the oblivion.' Later, he literally went through the agonies of hell, but firmly stood his ground with the conviction that the sun will set on the British Eempire within the next 50 years!

Current Situation and Analysis

1. Sunset on Atlantic World Order

Rise of Indo-Pacific World Order

For many long years, the relatively small-size nations in West Europe had colonised half the world. But with the end of the Second World War, the empires of European countries declined and were dissolved. It was then that the influence of Europe on international politics suffered an eclipse. But two factors saved them–on the one hand, US sheltered them while on the other, they decided to stick together. That is how the Euro-Atlantic world order could retain at least some of its influence. But then, Soviet Union disintegrated in 1991. This created an impression that USA would be left as the only Super Power in the world. So long as the Soviet Union was powerful, the US needed friendly nations in Western Europe. But this bond of friendship was subject to the sphere of influence of USSR. After it vanished from the world map as a mighty political entity, the US started feeling that it should be the only Super Power calling the shots in the world political arena. This continued for about a decade. But 9/11 in the year 2001 witnessed Islamic terrorists launching a murderous attack on the Twin Towers of the World Trade Centre in New York. This suddenly woke up the US to the fact that Islamic terrorism was knocking at its doors as a check on its unbridled powers. When US realised that Afghanistan had become the safe house for Islamic terrorists, its attention was diverted from the European scene to the Asian continent in a major policy shift. America decided to concentrate its attention on the Asia-Pacific region in order to destroy Islamic terrorism. Since Soviet Union had collapsed, the need to maintain a defensive wall against it in Europe had ended. Tracking sources of Islamic terrorism was the second decisive factor. Until 1991, Moscow was planting landmines of political challenges to the US in various real or potential battlegrounds. Thereafter, in the last three decades, Beijing has replaced Moscow as the mighty challenger to the US. Naturally, in order to counter the Chinese aggression, the US felt the need for paying special attention to the countries strategically located in the Indian Ocean and Pacific Ocean regions. There arose a new-found necessity to build bridges of friendship with such nations. The next factor was related to the economic

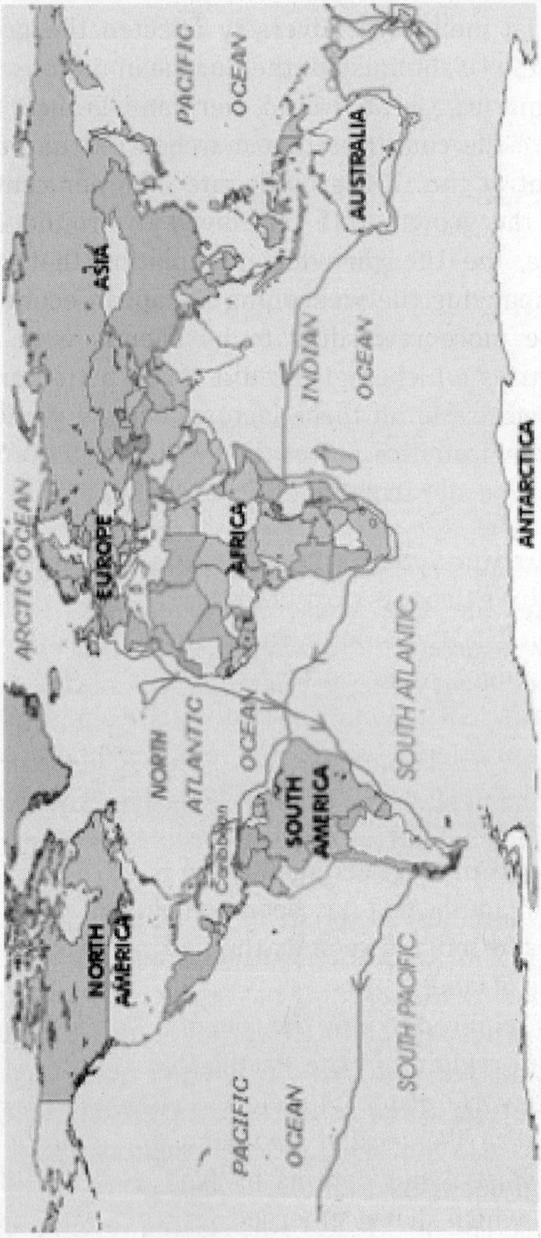

The decline of the Euro-Atlantic region and the rise of the Indo-Pacific region

crisis triggered by the fall of Lehman Brothers in 2008. This financial meltdown adversely affected the growth, not only of the US, but also of the European nations. Prior to 2008, America, Great Britain, Germany, France, Spain Canada were the countries that marched on the path of development at the GDP growth rate of 7 per cent, but post-2008, the growth rate nosedived to around 2 per cent! Hence, the US started contemplating that rather than accompanying the weakening European economies, it would be more rewarding to be friends with some Asian countries which registered a much better growth rate. It is because of all these factors that the pendulum of international politics is now swinging from the Euro-Atlantic world order to the Indo-Pacific world order.

2. Rise of Greater South Asia with India's leadership

In the three decades post Cold War, India has retained a favourable balance between economic growth and democratic polity. India's other achievements are sound law and order situation, successful implementation of L-P-G (Liberalisation, Privatisation and Globalisation) and a great leap forward in the fields of science and technology and defence. As a cumulative result, India has acquired a prominent and prestigious position in South Asia. In the same period, South Asia has been converted into Greater South Asia and India is seen as the natural leader of this vast expanse of land.

India is required to play the role of a link between the Indian Ocean region and the Pacific Ocean region in the Indo-Pacific world order. Therefore, it is imperative that India should strike cordial and amicable relationships with South-East Asian nations as well as other groups of nations which have emerged in this geo-political territory. If India can strike bonds of friendship with the Association of South-East Asian Nations (ASEAN), ASEAN Regional Forum (ARF), Asian Pacific Economic Community (APEC), etc., it will be a great relief for the post Cold War world. Fortunately, India has acquired a reasonably good reputation as a reliable nation in the Indo-Pacific world order.

On the one hand, India and greater South Asia are emerging as powers to reckon with, while on the other, the European Union is experiencing recession, both economic and political. It was way back in 1957 that six countries in Europe came together to sow the seeds of European Economic Community. Much later, in 1992, six more nations joined this community and European Economic Community was converted into European Union. In 2004, 16 nations in East Europe came under the umbrella of European Union, making it a group of 28 nations. Unfortunately, while the number of countries increased, the differences of opinion also started surfacing when the US attacked Iraq militarily, without adhering to the Security Council of United Nations. Some European countries, like France and Germany, opposed the US while some other countries came forward to support the aggression. As a later development, Islamic terrorism created fear among the European countries, with some European countries favouring 'nativism', which meant the original sons of the soil were to get first preference while the newcomers/migrants were to enjoy only secondary benefits. In this manner, what Maastricht Treaty forged together as European Union in 1992, is clearly seen on the decline in the last few years. All this definitely takes us back to the prediction by young Veer Savarkar about the change of tide.

3. Prevalence of Islamic Terrorism and Expectations from India

At the dawn of the 21st century, on September 11th, 2001, the Islamic terrorists launched a terrifying and gruesome attack on the Twin Towers of the World Trade Centre at New York in the US. The Twin Towers signified the World Trade Organisation. In other words, they were the symbols of world capitalism. The devastation caused by the Islamic terrorists underlined the fact that 'Marxism will challenge the capitalism of Euro-Americans' is a postulate gone horribly wrong. The capitalist nations and their philosophy had received a real threat from a non-economic factor, such as Islamic terrorism! In the last 20 years thereafter, Islamic terrorism has started threatening the very existence of several nations in the world. Shashi Tharoor has rightly described this as 'the present century is born in blood and baptised in fire.'

Of course the birth of the present-day Islamic terrorism is a 40-year old story. In 1979, Soviet Union entered Afghanistan with full military power. The US could not tolerate Soviet influence in this geo-strategic position. Therefore, to counter the Soviets, the US took the initiative and the strategy they deployed contained the origins of Islamic terrorism. In the 1980s, the US espoused the extremist religious elements (the *jihadis*) among the Muslims. They encouraged Pakistan to create a Sunni Islamic front to counter Soviet dominance in the region. It was a coincidence that in 1979, the Islamic revolution occurred in Iran, under the leadership of their supreme religious leader Ayatollah Khomeini. The anti-Soviet front, comprising Saudi Arabia, Pakistan and other countries displayed the might of Sunni nations. On the other hand, the Islamic revolution in Iran exhibited Shia power. All

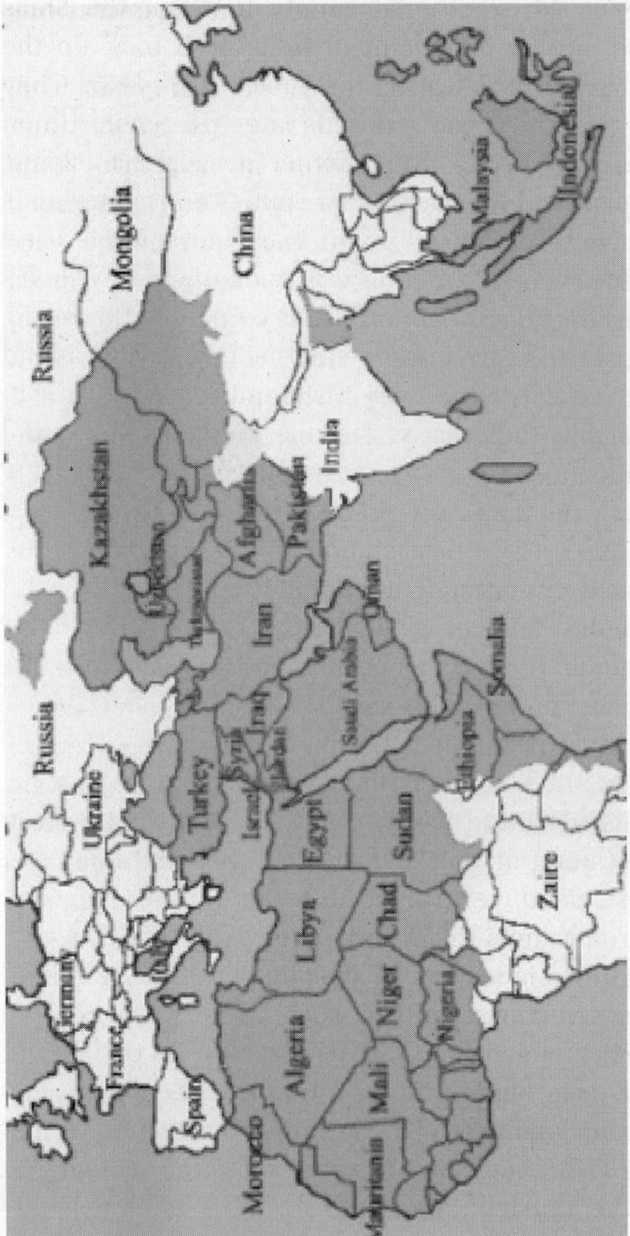

Islamic Countries

are aware of the traditional enmity between the Shias and Sunnis, but at that point of time, both took up the common agenda of defeating the Soviet aggression. They could achieve this target. A decade later, the Soviet Union itself disappeared and after another decade, the Islamic terrorists attacked America. As a result, Islamic extremists became convinced that Islam was indomitable and undefeatable. This declaration was enough for the *jihadis* to export Islamic terrorism to various corners of the world, wherein it started thriving and creating havoc. One should understand that Islamic extremists and *jihadis* desire to establish *Shariat* law, that is the rule of Allah all over the world. Therefore, it is not enough for them to finish the Marxist and the capitalist States but also the reformist Muslim leaders. The official standpoint of *jihadi* Muslims is to eliminate every other contender in front of them.

For the last few years, Islamic State (formerly Islamic State of Iraq and Syria) has been trying to hold the entire world to ransom. It has spread its tentacles in the entire West Asia and North Africa. Islamic State is a sect of Islam. It was established by Abu Bakr al-Baghdadi, a *jihadi* leader. He established Sharia law in Syria and declared himself to be the Khalifa of the Islamic State. He encountered a rival Islamic *jihadi* sect called Al-Qaeda. Its leader Ayman al-Zawahiri became the sworn enemy of Abu Bakr al-Baghdadi. In the later years, Baghdadi emerged victorious, hence other terrorist outfits, such as Boko Haram, Al Nusra also extended hands of friendship to Baghdadi. In the recent past, Islamic State is trying to consolidate its position in Afghanistan. On the other side of the fence, in April 2017, Saudi Arabia was successful in bringing 39 Islamic countries together to form a Sunni front and raised a common Army under the leadership of General

Rahil Sharif, the former Chief of Army Staff of Pakistan. This led to a reaction from Shia Iran which raised its arm against the Sunni conglomerate. In conclusion, all these developments have led to a ghastly series of sectoral and tribal wars, racist armed strifes, mass killings and other forms of bloodshed, from the Mediterranean Sea right up to River Sindhu.

1. Leon Panetta

America has realised that it is necessary to develop a cordial relationship with India and to make India better equipped from the armament point of view, for keeping a check on China in the Indo- Pacific region. In June 2012, the then Defence Secretary of US, Leon Panetta visited India. During his speech in New Delhi, he made a very significant statement, 'We desire that the strategic relationship between US and India should become deeper and more comprehensive. We wish to go beyond the conventional relationship of US as an exporter of armament and India as its customer. Our policy in times to come would be that of higher-level co-operation for research, development and production of armament as joint projects between the two countries. Going this way would help India acquire the latest defence equipment (Devin Hegarty, 'The Indo-US Entente' in *Engaging The World*, p. 145).

Leon Panetta also announced to the world, as early as 2011, that 'America will henceforth accord more importance to the Pacific Ocean than the Atlantic Ocean. By the year 2020, 60 per cent of the American naval fleet will be deployed in the Pacific and 40 per cent in the Atlantic.' This clearly indicates the process of Indo-Pacific region occupying the centre of the world. It also makes it clear that America and Europe are giving more importance to India,

Japan and Australia as compared to others. China has been making strong inroads in the Indian Ocean as well as in Pacific. For keeping a tab on China's plans, America would be willing to enter into treaties of a comprehensive nature, including economic, political and strategic issues, with all the countries situated on the rims of these two oceans. Free trade and unhindered movement of Merchant Navy ships through both these oceans should be ensured. This is the new American maritime policy. After the end of the Second World War, it was necessary for Japan to impose certain restrictions on itself. However, Japan has now decided to cast away these constraints and to become more proactive in the Indo-Pacific region, specifically to arrest the demonic ambitions of China.

2. C. Raja Mohan

While describing and analysing the current situation, C. Raja Mohan has used the mythological concept of the great churning of the oceans in a very poignant manner. He says, 'In the Indo-Pacific region, India and China are locking horns for dominance. India represents the gods and China, the demons! Both are keen on getting the best rewards out of such great oceanic churning. America, like Bhagwan Vishnu, has come forward to support the side of the gods (Dr. Arunoday Bajpayee, 'New Great Game in the Indo-Pacific Region and India', in *World Focus*, December 2015, p. 75). Of course, one has to take into account that Donald Trump, the American President, has not been an apostle of reliable diplomacy and his initial position was that America should keep itself away from the affairs of the world. However, considering the challenges of the changing world order, the unavoidable nature of the circumstances may nail America in the Indo-Pacific region. Under these

India should lead greater South Asia: World Expectations

circumstances, when the Western world is receding and the Eastern world is rising in importance, the writings of Swatantryaveer Savarkar will easily attract one's attention owing to his accurate predictions of the future.

3. Ravindra Limaye

Having retired from the Indian Air Force as Air Vice Marshall, Ravindra Limaye has clearly charted out the boundaries of Greater South Asia in an article. He states, 'Afghanistan lies to the north of Greater South Asia, along with five Islamic countries in Central Asia: Kazakhstan, Kyrgyzstan, Tajikistan, Turkmenistan and Uzbekistan. The southern border of Greater South Asia touches the Equator. On the West lies the Persian Gulf while the Straits of Malacca lie on the East. The World expects India to lead this Greater South Asia. This means that India should become the guardian of Afghanistan which had once given asylum to Osama bin Laden and which has been the birthplace of several terrorist groups. The Euro-American world and many other countries also would like India to be the guardian of the five Central Asian Islamic countries. Several other Islamic countries which lie in the vast landmass, from the Persian Gulf to the Mediterranean Sea, treat India, not Pakistan, as a replicable model. Hence the world would expect India to establish very close relations with these countries too. Beyond the Straits of Malacca lies the Pacific Ocean. Through its partnerships with Pacific-rim countries, particularly in East Asia and South-East Asia, India should erect a strong front to counter the ambitious strategic position taken by China. This will ensure the safety and security of the Indian Ocean lying in the South. This too is an expectation of the world community' (R.D. Limaye, Need for a Collective Security, Arrangement in the

Southern Asian region, *Emerging Issues in Indian External Relations*, p. 157).

4. Hindman

During his stay in London, Savarkar used to write news features for newspapers based in Pune. Among them, a feature published on December 20th, 1906 in Pune is very notable: British socialist leader Hindman had given a lecture in London. This news feature has covered it. The topic of the lecture was Russia's defeat by Japan. Hindman mentioned that the self-awareness and vivacity that this victory created in Japan, has also reached China. He told the audience that the entire Asian continent is now brimming with a vivacious spirit. This vigour and vitality will ultimately result in the independence of India and all other Asian countries, was the prediction of Hindman. He also told the audience enthusiastically that 'ultimately it is the efforts of the Asian people that will cause the great Asian revival of fortunes.' It is significant that Savarkar covered this lecture and reported its essence to Marathi readers. All of it is coming true after 114 years!

5. Mark A. Gabriel

Mark Gabriel is a thinker who has logically analysed and presented the *jihadi* standpoint and mentality. It all started with Kemal Pasha of Turkey adopting a secular attitude and obliterating Khilafat. Kemal Pasha got support from a few leaders in different countries. In strong opposition to such liberal and secular Muslim leaders, an outfit called Muslim Brotherhood was established in Egypt. Its aim was restoration of the rule of Allah. Syed Qutub, a very obstinate Muslim leader, became the philosopher of Muslim Brotherhood. He presented the philosophy of *jihad* and challenged all secularist Muslim rulers. The invasion of the World Trade Centre in New York on September 11th, 2001 has its origin in the *jihadi* philosophy of Syed Qutub (Mark A. Gabriel, *Islam and Terrorism*, p. 123).

Mark Gabriel was originally a Muslim, who took up this name for his own security after he got converted to Christianity. While he was still a Muslim, he studied Quran in depth and then taught Islam for a long time at Al Azhar University in Egypt. However, he got disgusted with the continuous indoctrination into violence for Islamic cause. He therefore relocated to another country and converted to Christianity. He has exposed many unpleasant truths in his book *Islam and Terrorism*, but it is important to note that the same truths were expressed by Veer Savarkar prior to Independence through his speeches and writings in a very blunt and outspoken style. He had said, 'Islam has always desired to create the Islamic rule all over the world by any available means.' Denying, underplaying or trying to cover this fact for political gains is not right, safe and acceptable, was the standpoint of Veer Savarkar. Today if one reads the book written by Gabriel, one will realise that the stance taken by Savarkar is getting vindicated today, through its wider acceptance. One should definitely read the speeches delivered by Savarkar in his capacity as the President of the Hindu Mahasabha. One would realise that Gandhiji always tried to present that there was no problem of Muslims in India. Gandhiji's followers represented that the issue of Muslims was created by the British. No such problem existed in India before the advent of the British. The Leftists/Marxists and socialists blamed the poverty and ignorance of the Muslims and presented a naive optimism that with eradication of poverty and removal of ignorance, the Muslim problem would be over and gone! During that period of self-deception, Swatantryaveer Savarkar alone stated openly and clearly that the origins of the problem of Muslims were located in Islam! Today, most of the world has endorsed this stand of Savarkar!

6. Dr. Sarvepalli Radhakrishnan

In his book, *The Hindu View of Life*, Dr. S. Radhakrishnan has properly analysed the sectoral and racial violence in the Muslim world. When Islam itself claims that it is the sole proprietor of truth, it often happens that some sects of Islam come up with the same claim. After some more time, another upstart surges forward to declare that he is the true owner of the entire truth. Under these circumstances, the rival claimants inevitably take recourse to armed struggle and bloodshed to prove their superiority! Dr. S. Radhakrishnan has stated an important principle in his book: 'Those who love their sect more than truth, end by loving themselves more than their sects' (*The Hindu View of Life*, p. 37).

□

15

Friends and Enemies: Matters of Strategy

Thus Spoke Swatantryaveer Savarkar...

The 22nd session of the Hindu Mahasabha was organised in 1940 at Madurai. If we quote the thoughts expressed by Savarkar in his presidential speech, there will be no need to explain as to how relevant these are today: "The sanest policy for us which practical politics demands is to befriend those who are likely to serve our country's interests in spite of any ism they follow for themselves and befriend only so long as it serves our purpose" ('*Hindu Rashtra Darshan*' in *Selected Works of Veer Savarkar*, vol. 4, p. 361).

Later, while delivering a speech at Jodhpur in 1956, Savarkar made it clear that 'he desires India to lend an unambiguous support to Israel' (*Savarkar Vichar Darshan*, p. 270).

Current Situation and Analysis

Major Changes in India's Foreign Policy

Pandit Jawaharlal Nehru initiated and nurtured independent India's foreign policy in the beginning. In later years, the policy underwent a notable and major change. The speed of transformation in the policy has increased multifold since 2014, partly because the global scenario has transformed itself in the post-Cold War period. Particularly after 1991, China started becoming very ambitious with the objective of stonewalling the American influence and even challenging its status as the only Super Power of the world. China did its best to stand on its own as a power centre and started enhancing its network to cover and include several countries of the world. Therefore, before talking about our policy and the changes therein, we must throw some light on this ambitious strategic plan of China. When Mao Zedong was the Premier of China, the Chinese policy had two major foundations: create a socialist national structure on the one hand and chart out a foreign policy which would be supportive of the internal socialist structure. Though the label was that of socialism/ communism, what has actually prevailed in China is a very militant nationalism. The present President of China, XI Jinping, has in front of him a very clear goal of upscaling the standard of living of the Chinese people. To achieve this, he wants to expand Chinese trade throughout the world. Hence, his current foreign policy has been shaped to achieve extension of political and economic influence over all the continents. A major example of this policy is the 'One Belt One Road' programme undertaken by the ambitious high command of China. Under this programme, China wants to create a trade route on land as well as on oceans. The former Foreign Secretary of India, Shyam Saran had a very pungent comment to offer on this strategic programme of China: 'This strategy is like an orchestra launched by China, by including singers and instrumentalists from a number of countries. However, the basic condition of China is that the songs of this orchestra should be Chinese. Their words, tunes, music, rhythm, everything should be Chinese!'

The highway that China is planning to construct connects the Pacific Ocean with the Baltic Sea. It goes through Central Asia, Russia and Baltic countries to connect Asia with Europe. The other one is the maritime Silk Route which has the Yellow Sea, East China Sea, the Gulf of Taiwan, South China Sea in its stride. It then crosses the Straits of Malacca and enters the Indian Ocean. The Indian Ocean has its spread right up to Djibouti port in North-East Africa. So the Chinese maritime route also reaches up to Djibouti. One more maritime Silk Route will commence in China and going through Pak-occupied Kashmir, it will reach the Gwadar port of Pakistan. After this leg of surface travel is over, the route will enter the Arabian Sea. China also wants to build one more road to the far east of India upto Kyauk Fu port of Myanmar. This road will enter the Bay of Bengal.

The maritime Silk Route planned from East China to the North-East through Yellow Sea and Straits of Malacca can be clearly perceived as a trap to arrest the sphere of Indian influence in this region. Vietnam lies on the left of this maritime Silk Route, while Philippines is on the right; to the South is Indonesia. To the North of the Straits of Malacca lies South China Sea in which China has drawn a 'nine dash line' in the shape of the English letter 'U'. China has declared that the portion of South China Sea up to this 'U'-shaped line belongs to China. A claim under dispute!

The matter was referred to the International Court of Justice at The Hague. The Court declared the nine-dash line of China as illegal and untenable. However, China has refused to bow to the decision of the International Court too! So the situation is that China forcibly entered the Indian territory in the Himalaya in 1962 and illegally occupied some portions. It continues to claim that Arunachal Pradesh, a state within India, belongs to China! In addition, Gilgit

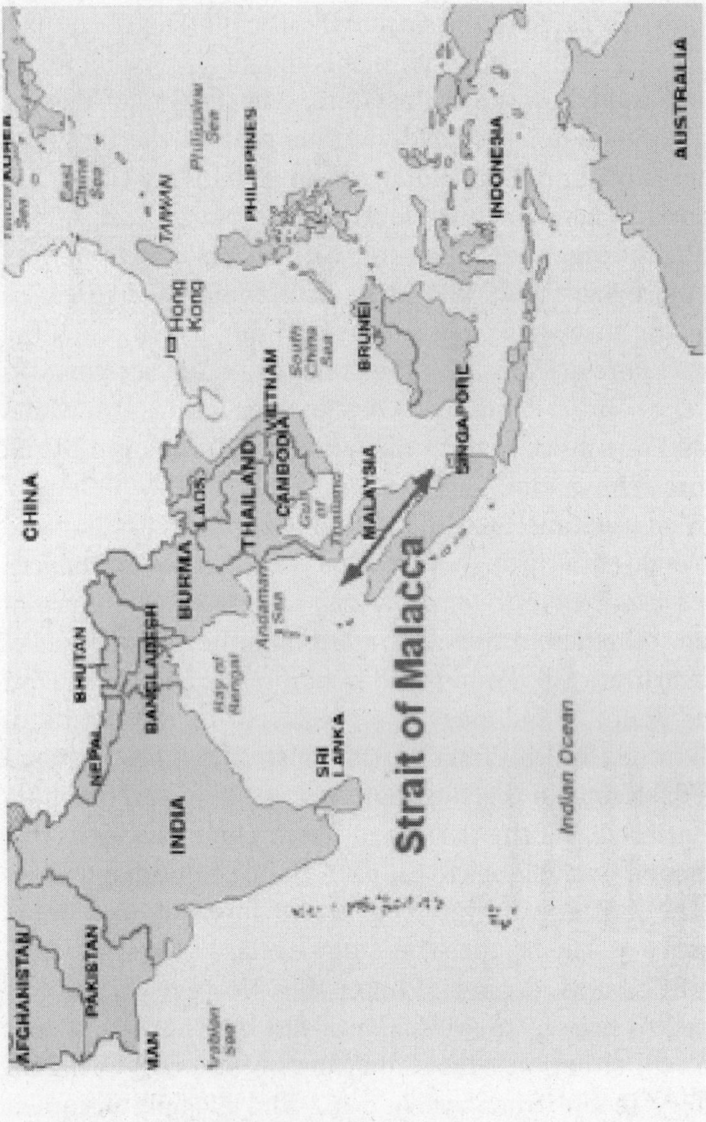

Straits of Malacca

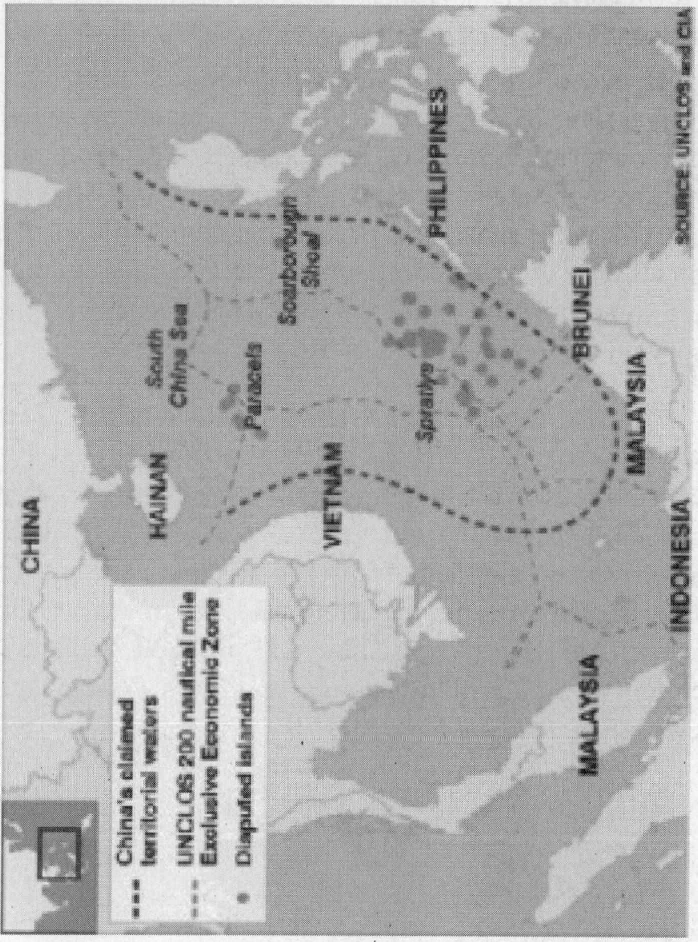

China's monstrous ambitions

and Baltistan in Pak-occupied Kashmir have almost been usurped by China under the name of economic corridor. Now it is probably preparing for an aggression from the East through the oceanic route.

In this background it is so natural to remember Swatantryaveer Savarkar. His autobiographical book *Majhi Janmathep* (My Life Imprisonment) offers enough evidence of his long-term vision. Savarkar stepped into Andaman in 1911, as a prisoner with two life imprisonments on his head, totalling 50 years! But even while stepping into the jail, he was not worried about what would happen to him. He was contemplating about the safety and security of his motherland even at that point of time!

Senior's View
Samir Saran

Looked at from the Indian point of view, China is clearly planning to encircle India under the garb of the so-called Silk Routes! In the eyes of Samir Saran, a thinker, 'Particularly in Pak-occupied Kashmir, the unholy alliance of Wahabism of Pakistan and Han race of China will probably make life difficult for people of all other sects and races' (Wahabism meets Hanism, *Times of India*, p. 16).

□

16

Naval Preparedness of India

Thus Spoke Swatantryaveer Savarkar...

After the newly born Jew nation, Israel, came into being, Savarkar welcomed it whole-heartedly on December 19th, 1948. During the same speech, he lambasted the policy of the Government of India towards Israel in strong words: 'Ms. Vijayalakshmi Pandit, who represents India in the United Nations, has reportedly expressed a view that the creation of Israel has stabbed the unity and integrity of the State of Palestine. Actually today's rulers of India are the same people who stabbed the unity and integrity of India by consenting to its Partition and creation of Pakistan. What can be more comic than the sight of the same persons shedding tears on the division of Palestine?'

Current Situation and Analysis

Any sensible person will easily conclude that about 70 years after the ridiculous action of denouncing Israel, the present rulers of new India have now come out with the right policy towards it.

Savarkar was a great visionary. Even at the threshold of entering a double life imprisonment, this courageous leader dreamt of the creation of a naval fortress to protect India. Though late, his dream has come true.

When we talk about our foreign policy and the changes that have taken place in it in the last 70 years, there are two significant interpretations of the construction of a sea-fort in Andaman-Nicobar in the eastern sea. The first is that we acted with the motive of nurturing an Ocean-oriented mindset in India; the second is that we gave an eastern orientation to our foreign policy. In the case of both these topics, remembering Savarkar is inevitable.

On November 26th, 2008, Mumbai was brutally attacked by our enemies entering from the Western sea-route. This sudden attack gave us a burning awareness of how well prepared should be our Coast Guards as well as our Navy. Of course, prior to that there was an awareness of the importance of maritime trade routes, when we decided to implement liberalisation, privatisation and globalisation in 1991. When we accepted the policy of free trade with foreign countries, we realised that 40 per cent of our world trade happens through the oceans. We also realised that if our merchant ships should ferry safely and efficiently, the Indian Navy should always be poised in the striking position. That is why we organised our first international naval fleet exercise in Mumbai port in the year 2001. We invited the Navies of 29 countries to participate in this naval exercise. However, whatever precautions we took were probably not sufficient. That is why we suffered a gruesome attack on Mumbai through the sea route on November 26th, 2008.

BJP established its government at the Centre in May 2014. After that, on February 7th, 2016 we organised our second international naval fleet exercise in Visakhapatnam port and invited the Navies of as many as 52 countries to participate in it. China has drawn a 'nine-dash line' in South China Sea and announced to the world its naval prowess. It has shown the audacity of ignoring the directions given by the International Court of Justice at The Hague. This arbitrary and oppressive behaviour of China has naturally caused deep anguish to many countries, like Vietnam and the Philippines. The show of strength undertaken jointly by the Indian Navy at Visakhapatnam was one way of giving some psychological relief to nations like Vietnam and the Philippines. Since ancient times, Indians have known proverbs like 'जलं यस्य, बलं तस्य' (power rests with the one who controls the waters). The modern display of this ancient proverb was witnessed by the world through the show of strength on our East-coast port of Visakhapatnam.

Nature has gifted India with a magnificent sea coastline of the length of a whopping 7,500 kms. K.M. Panikkar, reputed scholar-diplomat, had mentioned about 70 years ago that the future of India was closely linked with naval supremacy. Pandit Jawaharlal Nehru had also opined that the country which will control the Indian Ocean will impact not only Indian trade but also the sovereignty of India. Unfortunately, these thoughts were never acted upon. That is why on February 7th, 2016, Prime Minister Narendra Modi told the Indian marines, 'We are going to protect all the three seas which encircle India, because we know that only such vigilant guarding of the seas will provide a safety net for the prosperity and sovereignty of India.' In the naval fleet exercise of February 7th, the Indian Navy proudly displayed its frigates which could evade the enemy's radars, modern-day destroyers and speedy warships including those that carry fighter planes. A special feature was that most of them were made in India!

□

17

Andaman: A Marine Fort

Thus Spoke Swatantryaveer Savarkar...

Veer Savarkar stepped into the port of Andaman in 1911. He was sentenced with two life imprisonments, which was a gory prospect. But since he had vowed to sacrifice his whole life and everything at the feet of Mother India, even while entering the jail, he was contemplating the protection of the Indian soil at that critical juncture. The following extract from his autobiography, *Majhi Janmathep* is very expressive:

'The day we stepped into Andaman, I have got a feeling that Andaman is a marine–fort of India! In the future, India will establish its airforce station and naval base in Andaman, so that if at all some Eastern power dares to transcend its limits and tries to invade the territory of India, the first rock-solid resistance to its ambition will come from the marine–fort of Andaman, much before its warships and fighter planes think of touching the coastline of India' (*Majhi Janmathep*, part 2, p. 624).

Current Situation and Analysis

This Eastern group of islands of Andaman and Nicobar is like India's entrance door to the Eastern sea. If these islands are not within the sovereignty of India or if their fortification and ability to put up a fight is feeble, any inimical invasion from the East will directly knock at the door of Kolkata port. But if this group of islands is a part of India's sovereign territory and if it is fortified with the necessary airforce and naval armament, with a strong column of Indian Navy standing on guard, the invading warships of any Eastern enemy can receive their first blows of retaliation right at Andaman. It is perfectly legitimate for Andaman to be a part of India because its habitation and culture are completely Indian. Should we understand the geographical position of Andaman-Nicobar group of islands, we will be able to appreciate that as early as 1911, that is a century-and-a-decade ago, Swatantryaveer Savarkar had understood and underlined the colossal significance of these islands from the point of view of the defence of India. The Chinese Navy can enter the Indian Ocean from the Gulf to the East of India. Andaman-Nicobar group of islands is located to the North-West of Malacca Straits. Savarkar had expressed his expectations of fortifying Andaman-Nicobar as the prospective airforce and naval base of India as soon as he entered Andaman. It was 90 years later that on October 8th, 2001 the Government of India established its Andaman and Nicobar Command and put up the posts of all the three defence wings–Army, Navy and Airforce. Later, on February 5th, 2010, the Government of India displayed a show of strength in the Asia-Pacific region, by organising '*Milan*', a combined naval fleet exercise of Navies of 12 countries, including Australia, New Zealand, Philippines, Thailand, Indonesia, etc. Thus, the Indian government fulfilled the expectations of Savarkar in the first decade of the the 21st century! (*Times of India*, February 6th, 2017, p. 14).

As Prime Minister of India, Narendra Modi accorded a great deal of priority to the construction of roads, bridges

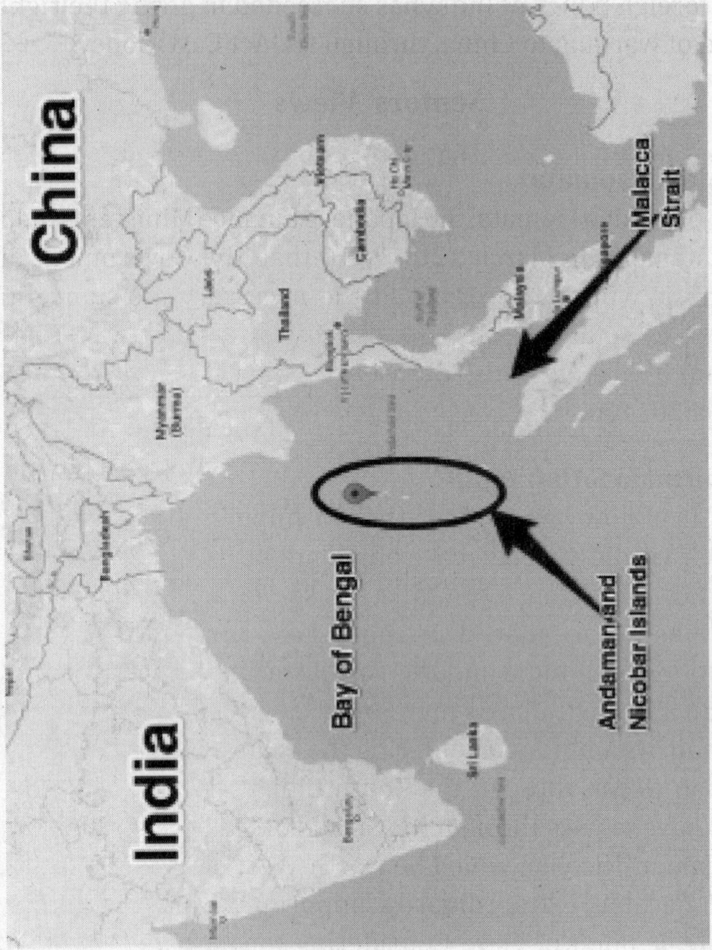

The importance of the Andamans

and tunnels on the Andaman and Nicobar Islands. He also announced that this construction project would be completed out of Japanese investments. In this manner, the foreign policy of India has succeeded in giving the right kind of warning to China, through its 'Act East' policy.

Seniors' Views

1. Akiyo Isomata

Mr. Akiyo Isomata, the Japanese Finance Minister issued a statement on March 12th, 2016 that 'the Government of Japan is willing to extend all the necessary assistance in order to establish the connectivity of Andaman-Nicobar group of islands with South-East Asia' (*The Hindu*, March 13th, 2017, p. 13).

2. Nirmala Sitharaman

It is now self-evident that XI Jinping, the Premier of China, is going to play more obstinate cards in international politics. This stance of China has so alerted the American administration that it is now keen on enhancing its relations with India and the Far Eastern countries, such as Japan and Australia. As mentioned earlier, if China does not contain its ambition of entering the Yellow Sea and then the Indian Ocean through the South China Sea, its naval fleet will have to pass through the Straits of Malacca. As a result, Andaman-Nicobar, which lie North-West of Malacca Straits will become extraordinarily important from the Indian strategic point of view. Considering this, the then Defence Minister of India, Nirmala Sitharaman spent the Diwali of 2017 at Andaman-Nicobar. Obviously she did not go there for a picnic! She went to take cognisance and review of the presence of all the three wings of Indian defence forces at Andaman-Nicobar. She also reviewed the striking and defensive abilities of our Navy, Army and Airforce. *Indian Express* published a news report on October 19th, 2017 on the Andaman visit of our Defence Minister: 'India's present foreign policy has become even more East-oriented. In the light of this policy reform, we should further strengthen our defence forces' presence in this area. India also feels the acute need to continuously watch the happenings in the South China Sea.'

The recent appointment of the former Indian Naval Chief Admiral D.K. Joshi as the Lieutenant Governor of Andaman-Nicobar is an important step in furtherance of the East-oriented action plan.

This is enough to prove what vision Swatantryaveer Savarkar possessed as early as in 1911!

□

18

Significance of Groups of Islands

Thus Spoke Swatantryaveer Savarkar...

'When India lost its sovereignty over small groups of islands, like Lakshadweep and Maldives, on the Western coastline, it was almost a cakewalk for European marine powers to knock directly at the doors of Mumbai and Goa. The then political powers-that-be could do nothing to detain the invaders away from the coastline' (*Majhi Janmathep*, part 1, p. 324).

'Now, at least in the future, we should correct this mistake. We still have other islands, like Lakshadweep on the West coast. We have Sinhaladweep to our South and Andaman Nicobar group of islands on the East coast. We should convert all these into our strongholds in the form of marine forts with adequate armed forces stationed therein. It is merely a political coincidence that today Singapore is the main checkpost of the Indian Ocean. The real natural security gate should have been Andaman, because Andaman, like Sinhaladweep, is the natural and cultural part of India' (ibid).

'Our capacity for a naval battle is still so crippled that the expansive modern coastline of India, ranging from Sindhu Sagar (Arabian Sea) to Hind Mahasagar (Indian

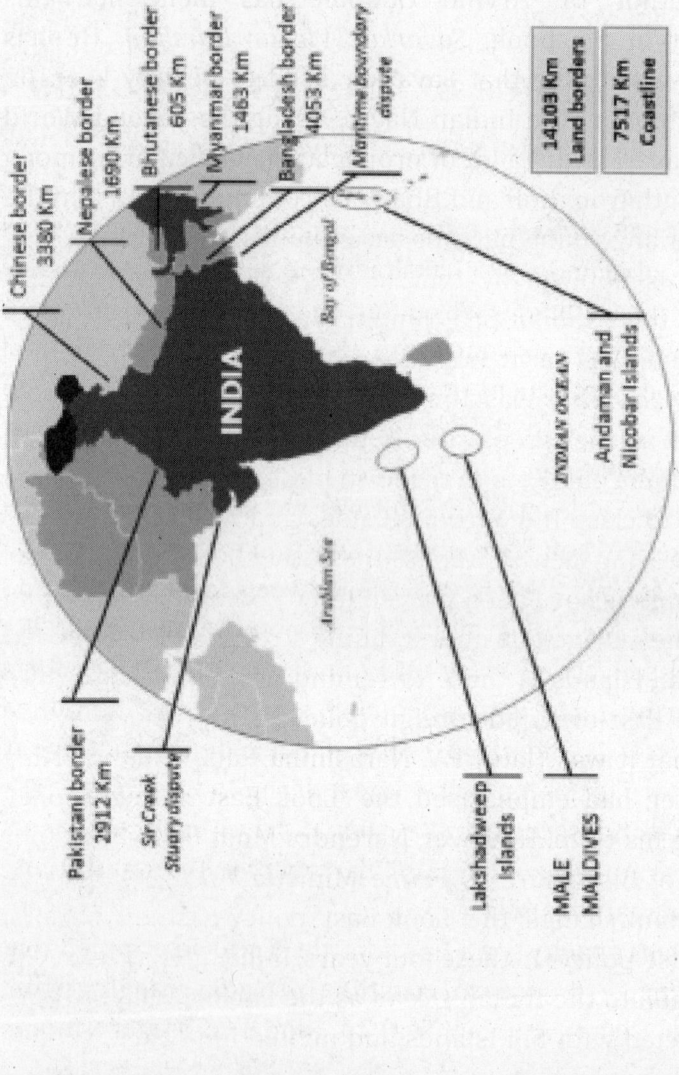

The archipelago that protects India

Ocean) and from Hind Mahasagar to Ganga Sagar (Bay of Bengal) is open to enter and hence completely insecure' (*Collected Works of Savarkar*, vol. 8, p. 500).

Current Situation and Analysis

Author Dr. Arvind Godbole has mentioned this extract in his book, *Savarkar Vichar Darshan*. He has added a footnote that Savarkar used to be very keen on strengthening the Indian Navy. During the Second World War, Savarkar did a lot of propaganda, particularly among the youth from Koli and Bhandari communities to join the Navy. Many young persons accepted his advice also.

It is noteworthy that in this extract, Savarkar has called the Arabian Sea 'Sindhu Sagar', whereas for Bay of Bengal, his term was 'Ganga Sagar'. This extract tells us that Savarkar was almost feeling thirsty to defend and protect all the three water bodies encircling India. Today, when Rahu and Ketu in the form of China and Pakistan are trying to clasp India from all sides and when Indian Navy is increasing its war preparedness, the thoughts expressed by Savarkar have been proven to be completely relevant.

The marine fort now standing strong at Andaman and Nicobar Islands is there to remind us of the importance of the East-oriented foreign policy of new India. It is a fact that it was (late) P.V. Narasimha Rao, who, as Prime Minister, had emphasised the 'Look East' foreign policy during his term. However, Narendra Modi in the first four years of his tenure as Prime Minister brought about an important change: the 'Look East' policy has now become 'Act East' policy! In these four years, India has paid as much attention to the Indian Ocean as the Pacific Ocean. We re-connected with Fiji Islands and invited important oceanic countries, like Australia, Japan, Vietnam, the Philippines and Indonesia to forge bonds of friendship with us. In ancient times, India had friendly ties with countries to our East and South-East. We are now replicating that successful model.

□

19

Foreign Policy

Thus Spoke Swatantryaveer Savarkar...

A session of the Hindu Mahasabha was held at Kolkata in 1939. In his presidential address, Savarkar expounded on the necessity of East-oriented foreign policy and action programme. The implementation of his ideas started 78 years later! This is an extract from his speech:

'Towards our neighbouring states of Burma and Tibet on the Eastern and North-Eastern frontiers, our policy will always be, so far as possible, of whole-hearted friendship and if they choose, even of a political alliance. They are our co-religionists and our political interests too are not inherently antagonistic. Nay, we will only find in general our mutual political strength augmented, if we continue to be political allies' (*'Hindu Rashtra Darshan'*, *Selected Works of Veer Savarkar*, vol. 4, p. 300).

Current Situation and Analysis

As a part of his endeavour to act in an East-oriented manner in the external affairs arena, Narendra Modi has eulogised Buddhism. He has underlined the fact that India has had deep-rooted cultural relations with the Eastern countries since ancient times. He has established a special sister-city relationship between Kyoto in Japan and Varanasi

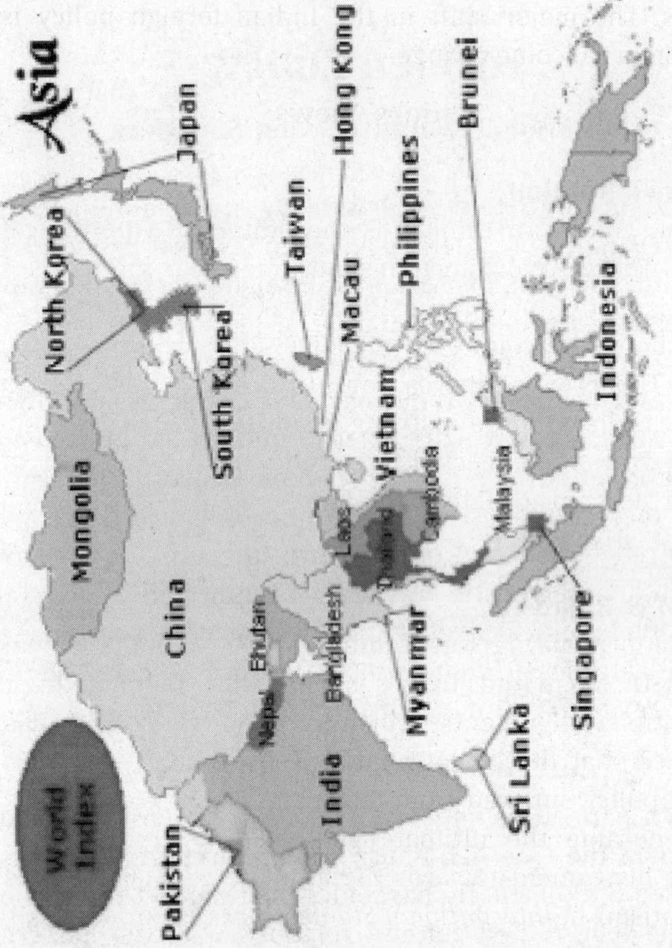

Eastward-bound foreign policy

in India. This action can be easily said to be inspired by the guidance of Savarkar doctrine.

India's present East-oriented policy and action plan have received appreciation from the US. Such a quadrilateral partnership will be very effective as a strategy in operating the necessary checks and balances on the expansionist powers. The major shift in the Indian foreign policy is therefore a welcome change.

Seniors' Views

1. David J. Rothkof

This American thinker is the editor of a periodical *Foreign Policy*. According to his judgement, the intention of the US is that China's expansionist project of 'One Belt One Road' should be countered effectively in the Indo-Pacific region. That is why America wants to align with India, Japan and Australia to forge a strong quadrilateral partnership. Donald Trump is expected to include South Korea also in this partnership at a later date (*Times of India*, January 2nd, 2017, p. 12).

2. Dr. M. S. Rajan

The former Director of Indian School of International Studies, Dr. Rajan finds India's journey from non-alignment to multiple alignments worth a deep study. He has remarked that during Jawaharlal Nehru's regime, India's foreign policy suffered from fetishism. The non-alignment policy became the ultimate goal instead of remaining only an instrument towards the ultimate goal ('A Plea for Pragmatism', in *International Studies*, July-December 1978, p. 836).

Fetishism is originally a Marxist concept which represents an illusion that the instrument is the goal. Here is an example: human beings started using money because some instrument was essential for exchange of goods and services between two human beings. Since ancient times, different currencies were used. Initially, animals were the currency to be replaced by pieces of leather and then by pieces of some metal. Still later, we started calling pieces of paper, money or currency. This means money or currency is only an instrument for exchange of goods and services. However, now money seems to have become the objective of human life. Majority of the human race today gives utmost importance to getting and hoarding currency throughout their active life. Thus, an instrument has become the ultimate objective. This is fetishism. India faced such fetishism when China crossed into Indian territory in October 1962, challenging the sovereignty and integrity of India. Naturally, the dilemma was whether India should still stick to and preserve its non-alignment policy or whether protecting its sovereignty was more important! When we approached the Western countries for military and other aid, the dilemma or illusion was over and protection of sovereignty was clearly realised as the ultimate objective.

□

20

Neutrality of the Weak is Meaningless

Thus Spoke Swatantryaveer Savarkar...

Savarkar contributed an article to the Diwali issue of a periodical, *Sahitya Laxmi* in 1964. He came down very heavily in it on the foreign policy of India prevailing then. Given below is an extract, which also indicates how his judgement was found correct five decades later.

'It is essential that we should procure and possess not only those weapons which the world knows today but also endeavour to discover and produce newer and more destructive armaments through hundreds of laboratories and factories throughout the nation. With this exercise, when you become all powerful, that would be the right time to announce to the world that you wish to remain neutral or that you will not be the first to strike. Your decision to abstain from armed struggle will have some meaning and importance only then. Today, when the same words are uttered by you, the feeble and the weak, they are meaningless' (*Savarkar Vichar Darshan* by Dr. Arvind Godbole, p. 267).

Current Situation and Analysis

During her 11-year tenure as the Prime Minister, Indira Gandhi displayed much sagacity through her policy of non-alignment. She set our foreign policy free from the entanglement of moral theories and fetishism. Later, the Janata Party government with Morarji Desai as Prime Minister also did not follow the Nehruvian concept of non-alignment. It went in for genuine non-alignment. After the Cold War period got over, we went ahead with a nuclear power treaty with America. After 2014, non-alignment became merely an ornament of our foreign policy. Actually, we have entered into several bilateral treaties with a number of varied countries, keeping in view the national self-interest. Practically, we have treated multiple alignments as our code word instead of non-alignment. The LEMOA, that is Logistics Exchange Memorandum of Agreement, between America and India signified our strategic handshake with the US and a major deviation from the foreign policy of the last 70 years. Against this background, when the non-aligned nations' summit was held on September 18th, 2016 in Venezuela, India was represented by the then Vice President, Mr. Hamid Ansari. It was significant that Prime Minister Narendra Modi kept his distance from the non-aligned summit. The next such summit also was attended by the current Vice President of India, Mr. Venkaiah Naidu.

The foreign policy of the present rulers of India scarcely shows any signs of ambiguity, naivety and weakness. What is acceptable now under the label of foreign policy is whatever will satisfy the pragmatic self-interests of India. Naturally, this policy is definitely influenced by the principle of 'responsive co-operation' as propagated by Savarkar in two consecutive sessions of the Hindu Mahasabha. In the 23rd session at Bhagalpur in 1941 and the 24th session at Kanpur in 1942, Savarkar explained the doctrine of 'responsive co-operation'. It meant that whichever country behaves in a friendly manner with India, India would give it an equally friendly response. On the other hand, if a country is antagonistic to the interests of India, we should try to teach such country a lesson through our actions. Going further, 'responsive co-operation' also includes limited co-operation even with an unfriendly country if it facilitates Indian interests. That is why the Modi government accorded priority to enhancing friendly relations with all our neighbours. Unfortunately, when Pakistan did not change its stand of obstinate non-cooperation, we circumvented Pakistan and tried to align ourselves with other South Asian countries. One can observe that at present, not only Bangladesh and Afghanistan but even Iran, all of which are Islamic countries, have almost boycotted Pakistan. When Recep Erdogan, President of Turkey visited India and offered to mediate between India and Pakistan on the issue of Kashmir, we clearly declined his offer, but at the same time said 'yes' to developing trade relations. India informed China in very clear terms that the economic corridor that China wishes to build through Pak-occupied Kashmir to reach Gwadar port in Balochistan, is completely unacceptable to India. In conclusion, whatever benefits India is clearly acceptable whereas whatever harms India is absolutely deplorable. This is the essence of the foreign policy of the present rulers of India and it is completely in coherence with the principle of 'responsive co-operation' as propagated by Savarkar.

Any discussion on the transformation in the foreign policy of India cannot be completed without talking about the present watchwords, such as 'surgical strike', 'hot pursuit', 'cold start' and 'no first use'. This is because the pro- and anti-remarks about these terms definitely remind us of Savarkar doctrine. On September 29th, 2016, Indian soldiers dashed into Pak-occupied Kashmir and destroyed a terrorist training camp. They killed 42 enemy soldiers and returned to the Indian soil unscathed. This surgical strike reminded the world of the bravery of Israeli soldiers, who had bombed the atomic reactors of Iraq, in 1981. This valiant act enhanced our national honour. Earlier in 2015, Indian troops had crossed the border of Myanmar to tackle the terrorists camping there in a hideout. This 'hot pursuit' became a glistening evidence of the transformation of our foreign policy.

In the last six years, the terms which were in circulation at the intellectual forums, the terms which evoked hot discussions–favourable and unfavourable–are the terms which not only exemplify the changes in the Indian foreign policy but also signify the pragmatic guidance given by Veer Savarkar.

India is currently passing through a challenging period. On the one hand, China is trying to surround India from all sides; on the other, Pakistan aided by China is trying to create obstacles in India's way. It is likely that Russia may also tilt towards this alliance. It cannot be guaranteed if America's new President Joe Biden will side with India. In such an atmosphere, India will have to be extremely cautious and continue its journey on the basis of pragmatic policies. It is important that the judgements of Veer Savarkar about the defence of India and the solutions suggested by him as early as 1950, are valid and applicable even today! Savarkar's thoughts quoted at the beginning of this section are definitely of much value in finding our way.

Seniors' Views

1. General Bipin Rawat

In January 2017, the then Chief of Army Staff, Gen. Bipin Rawat created a furore among several think tanks by his statement in an interview given to the periodical *India Today*. He stated that India had not crossed out the strategy of 'cold start'. It would be necessary to explain this concept. It was first discussed in detail in the Indian Army in the year 2004. Later in 2010, the then Army Chief Gen. V.K. Singh scored out the possibility by stating that 'no such strategy is being considered'. However, he also remarked that we can be more proactive to counter the inimical acts of Pakistan Army. On this background, when Gen. Rawat stated that this strategy is still alive, especially on the backdrop of the surgical strike, it was bound to come up for a hot discussion.

We have as our neighbour a country like Pakistan, which possesses nuclear power but nurses vile intentions and is supported by China. Hence an all-out open war may not be practical. Hence a 'cold start' is worthy of consideration. Under this strategy, our Army will cross the border to enter the enemy territory and occupy a small portion of it to use it for causing maximum damage to the enemy country. Before this mini-war is called off, we negotiate with the enemy on the basis of the occupied territory, finalise a deal that is favourable to us and then withdraw from this occupation back into our own territory. This is the meaning of 'cold start'.

'No first use' has also proved to be a stormy term. Following our nuclear explosion in 1998, India gave an open assurance to the world that it will not be the first to use nuclear weapons if at all it clashes with a nuclear power in the future. This led to the term 'no first use'.

2. (Late) Manohar Parrikar

In the Election Manifesto of BJP for the 2014 parliamentary elections, the voters could read an assurance of reconsidering the 'no first use' (NFU) policy. Later in 2016, the then Defence Minister, Manohar Parrikar made a bold statement that the 'NFU' concept was no more binding on India. Naturally there were repercussions, both favourable and unfavourable. But surprisingly there was more support for Parrikar than opposition. Our former Naval Chief Admiral Arun Prakash wrote an article in *Indian Express*, strongly supporting the stance of the Defence Minister. Rakesh Sood, a diplomat-thinker also expressed the opinion that a lifelong commitment to 'NUF' was uncalled for. Pakistan does not accept any restriction. 'Pak openly states that tactical usage of nuclear weapons is acceptable to them. Under these circumstances, if we bind ourselves to our own declaration of NFU, it would amount to accepting that Pakistan may go ahead and take the initiative. In other words, we will have to digest the bitter truth that Pakistan would attack India first with a nuclear bomb and cause unlimited devastation in India. We can also retaliate by using a nuclear weapon, but due to our self-inflicted moral restriction, even this retaliation will have to be greatly subdued. And we may still have to face an opposition from the international community. It must also be noted that when Defence Minister Manohar Parrikar stated that NFU as a concept is not binding on India anymore, he also said in the next breath that India is a responsible nation and will never forget its responsibility.

Mahatma Gandhi: Defending India is Vital

The standpoint that Savarkar always espoused was that India is our country and its independence and sovereignty should be protected by us at any cost. He used to clarify every principle based on the most practical criterion of 'nation first, nation's well-being first'.

Savarkar also subscribed to the 11 holy principles, such as non-violence and truth, but he had no doubt that even these principles could be sacrificed for the welfare and defence of the country. As against this, 85 years ago, i.e. in 1935, Mahatma Gandhi had gone to an extreme while celebrating the principle of non-violence. His viewpoint can be understood better from this excerpt from his writing: 'The true non-violence lies in satisfying the craving for violence. If cows were intelligent enough, they would have understood that if they continue to feed themselves in large numbers to a tiger, ultimately the tiger will develop a nausea for beef. As a result, the basic nature of a tiger will change' (Sheshrao More, *Savarkarancha Buddhiwaad: Ek Chikitsak Abhyas*, p. 304).

Gandhiji had to soon amend this extremist outlook towards non-violence. He also had to acknowledge that defending your country is an important value and even going to war was acceptable for national defence. Now Gandhian thinkers also underline the fact that Gandhiji's thinking kept on evolving. Look at the viewpoint of Milind Bokil: 'When Kashmir was attacked by Pakistan in 1947, Gandhiji told Nehru that sending Indian Army to Kashmir was inevitable.' Likewise when China attacked India in 1962, Vinoba justified going to war by saying, 'no country can tolerate such aggression. Hence India is fighting a holy war.' In conclusion, the basic standpoint of Savarkar was accepted by Gandhiji in 1947 and by Vinoba Bhave in 1962.

Of course, now nobody has any doubt whatsoever about the necessity to be always prepared for war and to be able to defend our country with the ultra-modern armament' (*Gandhi, Vinoba Ani Jaiprakash*, pp. 9-10).

It will be perfectly in order to conclude that with the changing times, the standpoint of Veer Savarkar about defending our motherland was endorsed by the common people and their leaders alike.

□

21

Let Hands Hold Self-knowledge and Atom Bomb

Thus Spoke Swatantryaveer Savarkar...

Defend the Nation with Atom Bomb

'Our strategic natural boundaries are beautiful, but many unfriendly people live beyond the borders. It is not possible to win their friendship by singing philosophical hymns. If we behave in a slovenly manner, we will lose all that we have earned. Henceforth, our political philosophy vis-a-vis foreigners should always be tit for tat. The world around us is aggressive and is glaring at us with atom bombs in its hands. That is why we should also make the best use of these opportunities that accrue from Independence. We should build a mighty Army that is prepared for self-defence with atom bombs in one hand and self-knowledge in the other. We should attack if the situation so demands.'

It is important to note that in 1950, when the Islamic bomb of Pakistan was nowhere on the scene, Savarkar had underlined the need for India to make an atom bomb. (Savarkar Vichar Darshan P. 267)

Current Situation and Analysis

Savarkar was experiencing the evening shadows of his life when he completed writing his book *Saha Soneri Pane*

(Six Golden Leaves). He preached in this book that if our enemy is an insidious crook, India should become double the crook. In support of this dictum, he quoted two lines from the sanskrit poem *Kiratarjooneeya* by poet Bharavi. It is noteworthy that Lokmanya Tilak had quoted the same two lines in his magnum opus *Geeta Rahasya*. Thus while the *guru* cited ancient literature to explain the *mantra*, 'शठम् प्रति शाठ्यम्' (Tit for Tat), his worthy disciple also used the same lines for proving the same principle. These two lines are:

व्रजन्ति ते मूढधियः पराभवम्।
भवन्ति मायाविषु ये न मायिनः।।

(Those idiots who avoid being wily crooks in spite of knowing that their enemies are deceitful and crooked, ultimately end up being defeated).

Our dear motherland, India, needs both victory and wealth. So how to achieve them, how should we behave, are questions that the writings of Veer Savarkar can adequately reply.

No Armies can Kill the Truth

Anti-Hindutva brigade has always been criticising Modi government's policies, dubbing them as 'communal' and 'violence-prone'. But then, how can one fix the accountability for the dastardly attack on Mumbai by Pakistani pawns on November 26th, 2008? As Chief Minister of Gujarat, Narendra Modi had alleged that the policy of the Congress of appeasing the Muslims was responsible for the debacle. Recently, a book has been published corroborating this allegation. Its translation in Marathi has also been published.

R.V.S. Mani was working as Additional Secretary in the internal security department of the Union Home Ministry in 2008. Based on his own experience and information, he wrote a book titled *The Myth of Hindu Terror*, which created quite a few waves. Arun Karmarkar, the translator in Marathi, has written thus about this book: 'Ten Pakistani terrorists walked the distance of a few kilometres from the Colaba seashore to reach the designated targets. How could they exactly locate their target spots, such as Hotel Taj Mahal or Trident, Café Leopold or CST station? Did they find these spots without any local help or guidance? How could Ms. Chitkala Zutshi, the then Additional Chief Secretary of Maharashtra reach Hotel Taj exactly at that time? Why? How could she escape unscathed from there?' (*Weekly Vivek*, December 30th, 2018).

R.V.S. Mani has dared to ask these questions in clear terms! Here is a retired senior government officer hitting at the outdated policy of minority appeasement.

As many as 82 years have lapsed since the outspoken discourse by Veer Savarkar. We are actually experiencing the fact that no army can ever kill the truth, or '*satyamev jayate*'. There are dark powers which are now terrified and anxious that more of such gory truths will be exposed to the countrymen. That is why they have joined hands together in opposition to pro-Hindutva thinking and are trying to mislead the voters by hook or crook so as to reach the top seats of power once again.

Well-aimed Attacks

There is one more special feature of this book written by R.V.S. Mani. Surgical attack on Pakistan happened in September 2016 when Narendra Modi was the Prime Minister. A natural fallout of this attack was that the common Indian citizens felt elated and proud of the valiant Indian Army and of the firm decision-making ability of the pro-Hindutva leadership. However, the same surgical strike evoked a completely opposite reaction amongst liberal progressive thinkers in the country. They got extremely worried about their future if a vast majority of the Indians were to continue appreciating the daring acts of the pro-Hindutva leader of the country. Their anxiety led to their efforts to denigrate the achievements of the Army. One statement that came out was: 'Modi government did nothing new! Such target-oriented attacks had happened during the period 2006 to 2010 also!' The pro-Hindutva leaders have come to be treated like enemies and everything that they do is denigrated and denounced. With the help of a section of the media, a propaganda campaign was launched, stating that the Modi government has done nothing great compared to the earlier secular governments which had taken similar actions. However, R.V.S. Mani refused to believe such announcements and said in his book:

'Planning of such a target-oriented action or strike is done in a confidential manner. On all such occasions, a group of senior officials undertakes a minute and detailed study of the situation. The group also takes into account all the probable consequences of such an action. A plan is chalked out, covering the actions necessary to provide protection to the workforce and the armament to be used for such a strike. A detailed note is prepared, containing the sequential and detailed description of all the aspects of the action. Orders for such a study are issued by the top military command. A detailed division of responsibility and authority is prepared, specifying the roles of the two ministries involved, viz. Home Affairs and Defence. If one has to believe the statements of certain political leaders about similar surgical strikes having been done during the period 2006 to 2010, all the advanced preparation described hitherto had to be done on all such occasions. In reality, I have not seen any record of all these steps having been taken by the Home Ministry during the said period. This indicates two possibilities: either the then (UPA) government did not care to comply with the necessary process requirements before taking such important actions or some political leaders are profanely lying about having taken such actions. If the actions had really been taken, the leaders are not following the model code of conduct about secrecy of such actions or else their statements about surgical strikes being done by the UPA government were completely false' (Arun Karmarkar, *Hindu Dahashatvad Navache Thotand*, p. 126).

□

22

Savarkar: A Social Reformer

Thus Spoke Swatantryaveer Savarkar...

Savarkar invited eminent thinker-speakers, like G.M. Joshi, Chitrao Shastri and Divekar Shastri, to deliver public lectures at Ratnagiri. These turned out to be open house debates. Audiences from Ratnagiri could witness an intellectual tug of war between the reformers and the old-school thinkers or *Sanatanis*. Along with such public lectures, Savarkar continued his personal conversations with different people in order to bring about a change of heart. He tried to persuade the cobbler (Charmakar community) to allow and even encourage people from Mahar community to be socially friendly with them. Once Savarkar said this to Bhagoji Sheth Keer, 'I know that the orthodox people opposed you and prevented you from worshipping Lord Shiva because you belong to the Bhandari community. As a response, you constructed Bhageshwar Mandir! This was a great move! But now, why don't you do something to help our once untouchable brethren also to enjoy the pure spiritual pleasure? If you build a temple for them, your anger about orthodoxy can be called justifiable.'

Current Situation and Analysis

Savarkar remained stationed at Ratnagiri till June 17th, 1937. The British had imposed two bans on him–he could not cross the borders of Ratnagiri district and not engage in any political action.

But, after all, they were dealing with Savarkar! He proved by his actions that his spirit was always indomitable and it would be wrong to conclude that he turned to social work due to the restrictions imposed by the British. He became a social reformer not due to the circumstances but because social reforms were part of his nature. Savarkar always insisted that the feeling of the distinction of high and low social order and particularly the practice of untouchability should be obliterated. He also wanted to see women sharing the same privileges as men. In 1982, when he had not even completed 20 years of age, he wrote a poem expressing the grief of a widow and asking why were the doors for widow remarriage kept closed.

Social Work of Savarkar

It was in 1937 that Veer Savarkar presented a very logical discourse on his two principles: firstly, India is a Hindu nation and secondly, Indian politics needs to be Hindu-oriented. Majority of Indians responded favourably to his stand, but, 80 years after he had presented them. This positive response was overtly observed in the assembly elections in Uttar Pradesh. It must, however, be noted that behind this apparent political transformation, the prime movers have been the the workers of the RSS. These *Swayamsevaks* have been working for several years without expecting any personal gains. This led first to a socio-cultural transformation which proved to be a suitable background for political change. Swatantryaveer Savarkar also conducted social activities alongside political agitations, right from his young age. In fact, social reforms had always been close to his heart. This was because he knew intuitively that some time in the future the British Empire would have to relinquish its power over India. We would then be politically independent, but if our social and cultural spheres did not display equal dynamism as the political one, then such discrepancy would prove to be a challenge to India's independence. Savarkar reached Ratnagiri on January 6th, 1924 as a prisoner under house arrest. On June 17th, 1937, all the bans and restrictions imposed on Savarkar were removed and he was free to once again take flight like an eagle into the sky. But, even after being allowed to undertake political activity, his penchant for social work continued till the last days of his life. In other words, this great soul toiled all his life for fulfillment of objectives, like eradication of outdated traditions and customs and establishment of social justice and humanity. His social work during the Ratnagiri period was a great historic era in his life. Today, the social work that he had then undertaken has acquired outstanding importance.

It is admitted that even today the Indian society has not achieved complete freedom from age-old socio-cultural and religious customs and traditions. Even today, our mindset can easily turn to the orthodox practices. Even today, many of us do not display adequate sensitivity towards social justice or injustice, equality or inequality. Of course, in recent times, some good signs have been observed. Pro-Hindutva loyalists are trying to create an atmosphere which is congenial to social reforms through their own conduct and by undertaking new experiments. Unfortunately, many of our so-called progressive intellectuals are unable to appreciate the significance of Savarkar's social work and have been neglecting Savarkar consistenty and turning a blind eye towards his views on social reforms and his on-the-ground behaviour.

Concerted Efforts for Removal of Social Inequality

Savarkar had always been insistent on India becoming a highly developed and powerful nation in the world. He planned and executed several activities towards fulfilling his objective during his stay at Ratnagiri. He ran a campaign for the eradication of the evil practice of untouchability by encouraging entry into temples, dining together and other forms of living together by people from different social strata. In addition, he made serious efforts to propagate physical exercise, literacy, consumption of Indian goods and promotion of scientific temperament. On this path, he had to encounter stiff opposition from vested interests. For instance, many shopkeepers were unwilling to sell only Indian goods. The orthodox Hindus were staunchly against the so-called untouchables praying with them. Stubborn Brahmins and priests did not wish to allow the so-called lower social strata to study *Vedas* and other religious scriptures. Since Savarkar was busy building strong organisations of Hindus, some Muslim fanatics too detested him. Very often, even the common citizens did not support the spread of literacy and physical exercise. Savarkar even received personal threats, but he handled such antagonism with great diplomatic skill. For instance, some so-called high-caste citizens permitted the entry of Dalits in the outer area of temples but not into the sanctum sanctorum. Savarkar then had to compromise on his principles and was happy that at least the Dalit brothers and sisters could enter the temple complex and it marked a step ahead! Some orthodox and conservative persons were willing to dine with so-called low-caste Hindus but preferred to sit in a separate row! So, Savarkar allowed the lunch arrangement in different rows! When socio-religious get-togethers were organised specially for women, some upper-caste women declined to touch the Dalit sisters or apply turmeric powder and *kumkum* on their foreheads! As a via media, Savarkar asked his wife to conduct the actual task! Savarkar thus developed a practically wise style of functioning to take social reform movement further, even if gradually! Once a certain step was completed, he would start contemplating and planning on how to cross the next hurdle! He would often seek help from new friends, retain old friends and move gradually but firmly towards the final objective. Once he thought that Dalits could organise a musical band troupe to play at weddings, etc. As the Dalits were not financially strong to purchase the musical instruments, Savarkar helped them to obtain bank loans. He insisted on Dalit students sitting next to upper-caste students in schools without any discrimination. He even organised social workers' groups to keep an eye that this principle of equality was followed in schools.

All these experiments of social reforms needed publicity so as to create awareness among the larger sections of people. Savarkar himself wrote stories, poems, small plays and articles and arranged for their publication. He even listed seven bonds which restricted the activities of the Hindu society and these were:

1. Dalits banned from studying or reciting the *Vedas* and other religious scriptures
2. Ban on Dalits in conducting certain trades
3. The practice of Untouchability
4. Restriction on breaking bread together
5. Ban on inter-caste marriages
6. Disallowing entry of converts back into the fold of Hinduism
7. Not permitting journey across the oceans.

Savarkar identified these seven evils which

oppressed and chained the hands and feet of Hinduism and he did his best to break these fetters.

In the 1930s, Ratnagiri was the capital of the high orthodoxy in Hinduism. It was no mean task to propagate against such regressive thoughts and practices. A pithy comment on the thinking prevalent in that period is provided in a Marathi poem titled *Devachya daari* (At the Threshold of a Temple) by a famous poet of that period, Sopandev Chaudhari. It is a social poem which portrays a Dalit, say, Chokha, standing outside a temple because he is not permitted to enter it. He is very keen to see the idol of Lord Rama in the temple, to worship and light a lamp in front of it. But he is not allowed to do so. He then notices a Brahmin entering the temple and entreats him to conduct the prayers on his behalf. Watching this situation, poet Sopandev Chaudhari's heart fills with pathos.

Seniors' Views

Gopal Guru

Sometime ago, a symposium on 'Nationalism' was arranged at JNU, New Delhi with a few progressive speakers. The intention was clearly to launch a tirade against the concept of nationalism of pro-Hindutva followers. Naturally, the tenor of the speeches and discussions was like 'supporters of Hindutva care a hoot about the welfare of the downtrodden'; 'the only job of the pro-Hindutva thinkers is to continuously stoke a fire of hatred against the Muslims'; 'The ranks of pro-Hindutva leadership work only for the welfare of the so-called upper-caste Hindus' and so on. Now a book has been published carrying the summary of these lectures. It does not mention Veer Savarkar anywhere, but there is definitely a pathetic effort to undermine the contribution of Savarkar as a great social reformer. As an example, one can refer to the article by Gopal Guru, a professor at JNU. He has alleged that 'pro-Hindutva thinkers care only for the *parishkrit* (upper caste) Hindus without caring for the *'bahishkrit'* or Dalit classes.' Though the article is in English, the words *parishkrit* and *bahishkrit* have been used. If someone were to go through the pages of history with an objective view, he is sure to find that the topmost theoretician and commentator of pro-Hindutva thinking and the self-proclaimed representative of Hindu *rashtra*, Veer Savarkar, was clearly one of the greatest supporters of the underprivileged strata of the society. Savarkar had many a time invited the wrath and disdain of the orthodox upper-caste Hindus who felt that he invariably supported the Dalits. Even during the period of his house arrest, he toiled continuously to bring about a change in the social rank and position of the so-called lower castes and persuade the upper-caste Hindus to treat their deprived brothers with respect. To overcome this abject neglect of Veer Savarkar as a leading social reformer, some actions are required:

- The activities carried out by Savarkar should be explained and mentioned in different forums.
- Savarkar inspired a number of people to carry out activities that could eradicate the evil of social inequality from Hinduism. Information of such activists and their accomplishments should be communicated to the new generation.
- Bharat Ratna Dr. B.R. Ambedkar and many others had taken due cognisance of this yeoman role played by Savarkar. This fact needs to be duly communicated to the people.

- It goes without saying that communists, who took pride in calling themselves progressive had actually boycotted the *bahishkrit* classes, fearing the reaction of the *parishkrit* classes! These facts need to be highlighted with evidence.
- Savarkar deployed a multi-pronged strategy to bring about a total transformation in Ratnagiri district so far as social inequality was concerned, during the period 1924 to 1937. It should conveyed that a leading communist leader, Hiren Mukherjee played a leading role in publicising the strategy and contribution of Veer Savarkar in this field.

□

23

Eradication of Untouchability

Thus Spoke Swatantryaveer Savarkar...

Swatantryaveer Savarkar used to get agitated at the inhuman behaviour of the so-called high-caste Hindus towards the Untouchables. When he learnt that the Bhageshwar temple in Ratnagiri Fort area would be thrown open to the untouchables by its owner Shrimant Bhagoji Sheth Keer, Savarkar wrote a poem in Marathi, titled *Mala Devache Darshan Gheu Dya'* (Please Allow Me to See My God). At the main function, daughters of two scavengers sang this poem in front of the audience. To quote a few lines from the poem:

'मला देवाचे दर्शन घेउद्या।
डोळे भरुन देवास मला पाहू द्या।।
जो तुम्हिच करा दिनरात।
मळ काढित मळले हात।
म्हणूनीच विमल ह्दयात।
ह्दय त्या वाहू द्या।।

('Please allow me to see God. I must watch him to the delight of my eyes. We clean the world off the muck that's made by you. That dirties our hands, but our hearts are pure and clean. We offer our hearts as our gift to God!')

Current Situation and Analysis

We must Create a Paradise of Equality

Let us understand the deeper meaning of this poem to appreciate Savarkar's innermost feelings for the downtrodden. While writing this poem, he became so emotional that tears streamed down his eyes on seeing the upper-caste Hindus rejecting entry of Untouchables inside the temple, the abode of God. The ingratitude of the upper caste to the lower caste Hindus for their scavenging activities saddened his heart. Savarkar, Gandhiji, Malviyaji all spoke in one voice and were absolutely reasonable and correct. They all believed that if we were to get Independence without complete eradication of social inequality and untouchability, such independence would have satisfied only a few advanced sections of the society, but a large section of the Dalit community would have remained unhappy. Hence they considered it their duty to spread equality in India before it attained political freedom. They wanted all sections of the society to be in a position to enjoy the fruits of freedom and receive equal opportunity to walk on the path of self-development.

With this objective in his mind, Savarkar continued to work towards social reforms. A famous Maharashtrian poet of that generation, Narayan Muralidhar Gupte, also known as poet 'B', wrote a poem in Marathi, denouncing the half-baked Independence which does not give justice to the downtrodden. He criticises the upper-caste Hindus who opposed the movement for equality and humanity. He says:

ते स्वातंत्र्य खरे न, फक्त अपुली जे तोडिते बंधने।
अन्यांच्या पदशृंखलात रमते निष्कंप ऐशा मने।।

(That freedom which sets free only a few of us is not

real independence. What is the use of it if the others still remain in slavery?)

All these efforts of Savarkar were aimed at cutting off the seven bonds that fettered the feet of the society and prevented it from walking together on the path of progress. He did manage to gather round him some very close and dear colleagues, whose contribution helped in bringing social transformation in Ratnagiri district. Of course, his colleagues too had to incur the wrath of the traditional-minded friends and family members. Many had to quit their homes while some had to face censure at social, familial or communal levels. Some of them were ostracised by their kith and kin and by the conventional Brahmin priests. In spite of all this, these brave social workers did not drag their feet from the path of progress. They followed the path shown by their resolute and determined Guru Savarkar who could achieve a great deal. To illustrate this, a professor from Ratnagiri, Dr. Ramesh Kamble has narrated an anecdote in his book. He says,

'Dattopant Limaye, editor of the newspaper *Satyashodhak*, participated in a joint lunch programme arranged by Savarkar. Since he ate his lunch with Dalits, the orthodox people wanted him to observe penance. Since Limaye declined, the priests boycotted his family and stopped performing religious rituals for them. On this background, it was soon time for observing his father's first death anniversary. But the priests refused to perform the rituals at Limaye's home. As a solution, Savarkar deputed Moropant Damle as the priest to perform the rites. Limaye offered him 2 rupees 25 paise as *dakshina* (token honorarium) apart from a sumptuous lunch. Savarkar collected the contribution of one rupee from priest Damle to fund the Hindu Sabha! (Dr. Ramesh Kamble, *Social Work of Swatantryaveer Savarkar in Ratnagiri*, p. 38).

Imaginative Activities of Hindutva Loyalists

Drawing inspiration from Veer Savarkar, several Hindutva loyalists have implemented a variety of activities and programmes for the upliftment of Dalits in the last few decades. Two salient examples are that of Shripad Mahadev Mate and Anant Hari Gadre, though these are not all. Many others, like Kurtakoti Shankaracharya, Pachalegavkar Maharaj, Masurkar, Brahmachari Vishwanathji, Madhukarrao Deval, Madhavrao Kane, Bhaiyaji Kane, Girish Prabhune are some more illustrious examples. These and many more *karmayogis* have carried out selfless social work for the benefit of Dalits and Vanvasis (tribals) as if they personally owed a lot to the less-privileged section of the society. Savarkar himself inspired and encouraged Damle brothers, Nana Bapat, Bhalya Patankar, Salvi Guruji, Sawant Guruji, Wamanrao Chavan, Dr. V. M. Shinde, S. B. Khedekar and many others in their sacred exercise of social reforms. For doing selfless work consistently in public life, one has to develop a special mental attitude. Undoubtedly, Savarkar was an expert in developing such an attitude amongst potential colleagues.

Out of the workers mentioned above, one is tempted to write in more detail about Shripad Mahadev Mate, better known as 'Mate Master' and Anant Hari Gadre, better known as 'Jhunka Bhakar Gadre'! Mate Master gave tuitions in order to raise funds for of the upliftment of Dalits. He thus saved money through his personal efforts. Once he invited Mahatma Gandhi to his place of work, which was a slum area. Gandhiji was moving with great ease and comfort through the slum. This hugely appealed to Mate Master. In his Marathi book, titled *Upekshitanche Antaranga* (Inner Selves of the Neglected People), he writes a *shloka* (couplet) in Sanskrit about the objective of family life (*grihastha ashram*). It goes like this:

यथा वायूं समाश्रित्य सर्वे जीवन्ति जन्तवः।
तथा गृहस्थाश्रमाश्रित्य सर्वे जीवन्ति आश्रमाः।।

(The life span of human beings is divided into four sections. Just as all living beings live on the basis and strength of oxygen, the three other sections or *ashrams* of human life carry on with the help and support of *grihastha ashram*, that is, family life!)

Several Hindu loyalists utilised their own family life to bring into being social reforms and their inspiration was derived from Savarkar.

Communists: Preposterous and Incoherent Conduct

The movement for social reforms got a fillip in India from 1924, due to the initiative shown by several great personalities. Dr. Babasaheb Ambedkar started his public life in 1924 by taking up activities aimed at the betterment of Dalits. Narayanaguru in the South, Pandit Madan Mohan Malviya in the North, Mahatma Gandhi throughout India and Veer Savarkar under house arrest in Ratnagiri were some of the greatest sons of India, who were opposed to age-old and unjust caste system in India. The Communist Party had just arisen on the horizon of Indian politics. It, however, concentrated its entire attention on building up workers' unions in the light of the views of Marxism and Leninism. Their *mantra* was that the basis of all issues is economic, which can be resolved if 'red revolution' takes place under the leadership of the workers and if the right to private property is abolished. A total transformation can happen only then. So the comrades concentrated only on such actions. They firmly believed that casteism and the issue of social inequality created by birth-based castes were not the basic problems of India; the fundamental issue was financial inequality due to the capitalists as the exploiters and the workers as the exploited class. Once a decisive conflict happens between these two classes and once the exploited class eradicates the exploiters and takes the entire authority of the State in its own hands, it will automatically obliterate the caste-based inequality. In other words, the class conflict is the real foundation of the whole superstructure, so we should concentrate entirely on this foundation. The Communist Party continued fighting for the demands of the workers with such postulates where class conflict is considered the foundation and caste conflict as the structure built on the foundation. It is described as 'Base and Superstructure Thesis' in the Marxist scriptures!

Gandhiji and Savarkar as well as Dr. Babasaheb Ambedkar agreed *in toto* that the so-called upper castes in the Indian social structure had always been unjust to Dalits and it was necessary to transform the mindset of the upper castes to end this injustice. The *satyagraha* undertaken by Dr. Ambedkar at Mahad and Nashik in Maharashtra were based on this understanding, but the communists thought all this to be futile.

In the year 1929, textile-mill workers, unionised under the red flag of the Communist Party of India went on a strike. The communists wanted the Dalit workers also to participate in the strike and Comrade Dange visited Rajgruha, the residence of Dr. Ambedkar in Mumbai. Babasaheb listened to Dange but he knew that in any mill, Dalit workers were not allowed to enter the important weaving section because in this section of the mills, it was a common practice to use the workers' mouths for passing the thread from one worker to another. There was a popular misconception that even if one worker was a Dalit, the thread would become tainted with the saliva of his mouth. This would ultimately defile all the upper-caste workers in the chain. Therefore, Dalits were not allowed entry in the weaving department of any textile mill. Pointing out this discrimination, Dr. Ambedkar suggested to Comrade Dange that the long-standing demand to allow Dalit workers to work in the weaving department should be supported by the communist unions if the latter wanted the Dalits to join the strike. The communists did not accept this demand because they did not wish to displease many of the upper-caste workers. As a result, there was dichotomy between the Communist Party and the Dalit workers. In clear terms, the Communist Party supported the *parishkrit* or upper-caste workers and meted out injustice to the *bahishkrit* Dalits! This way, in 1929, the communist leaders and workers ignored the issue of inequality based on caste system and sided with the parochial upper-caste workers, while Veer Savarkar, Kurtakoti Shankaracharya and Mahamana Malviya were already taking by its horns the opposition of several upper-caste Hindus, to fight on behalf of the Dalits! Savarkar spent all his life on the basis of his *mantra* of placing the common good over and above the approval of the masses! (वरं जनहितं ध्येयं, केवला न जनस्तुतिः)

Now that seven decades have passed since Independence, one has to review the mindset of the masses and we find that we have not yet developed adequate sensitivity to think about social issues with a larger canvas in mind. Since every dark cloud has a silver lining, it is necessary to understand the social reform work done by

Veer Savarkar. It is therefore necessary to describe the hard realities of today.

An analysis of the present situation needs to begin with the unfortunate incident that happened at Khairlanji in Bhandara district of Vidarbha, a region of Maharashtra, in 2006. Four members of the Bhotmange family were brutally killed by a mob, after two girls out of the four victims had been blatantly raped. It is alleged that the women of Khairlanji also watched the rapes with unmoved eyelids. Later the four persons were stoned to death in cold blood. Their corpses were thrown into the canal and only one member of the family, Bhaiyalal Bhotmange, survived. He succumbed to a natural death in 2017. In 2014, three villages in Nagar district–Sonai, Kharda and Javkhed Khalsa–were witness to murders of seven Dalits. While it is murmured that the background to these murders was illegitimate relationships, the fact remains that human beings were eliminated in a beastly manner. Then in 2015, Indrajit Kulkarni and Megha Patil, a couple of Kolhapur was murdered by slitting their throats. Such incidents reached their crescendo when in Kopardi village, a 15-year girl was raped and brutally murdered by three youth. Out of all these incidents, the one in Kopardi village was somewhat different because the three rapists and killers belonged to the Dalit community, whereas the victim girl was from the upper caste. But in all these incidents, the common factors were that human mobs took law in their own hands and killed girls in a demonic manner, after making them victims of their carnal lust. Total lack of sensitivity is another common factor. Out of all these incidents, the killings at Kolhapur did not acquire a predominantly communal colour probably because both the victims as well as the murderers belonged to the so-called upper castes. So casteist attitude was probably not the most dominant factor behind that incident. Following the unfortunate incident in Kopardi, the Maratha community organised demonstrations condemning the brutality. Such demonstrations could be considered historic in their magnanimity in the post-Independence history. The Maratha community was non-reactive at the time of other incidents. It took to streets only after the Kopardi incident. It is also noteworthy that the majority of people from other unrelated castes remained mere spectators in case of all these incidents.

Seniors' Views

1. Sanjay Sonawani

'We are now being surrounded by poisonous elements. Khairlanji showed us a perverse face of human beings. Looking at it from anybody's point of view, it is a heart-wrenching incident. Whether the incident itself had caste implications or not is anyone's guess, but why was it given communal overtones? The girl at Kopardi village who lost her everything including life came from a poor family and was like the daughter of any of us. Why did it become necessary for the Maratha community to take to the streets to decry and deplore this perversity? Did the Dalit organisations not try to underplay it in the beginning? In case of the Kolhapur killings, nobody felt it necessary to take any stand! All this clearly suggests that our society is incurably and mortally plagued with communal feelings, which override human agony and misery. All groups decide on their stand on the basis of communal considerations. In that case, what social welfare do so-called social rebels and progressives talk about when they swear by the sacred names of Shahu-Phule-Ambedkar? We should ask this question seriously to ourselves'(Khairlanji to Kopardi: The Journey of an Agony',*Vivek* weekly, Mumbai, February 12th, 2017, p. 18).

2. Pandit Deendayal Upadhyay

When unholy incidents keep happening and when it becomes clear that their origins lie in psycho-sociological disorders, like hatred, lust and anger, it becomes a matter of worry. In this context, it will be useful to remember the philosophy of Integrated Humanism expounded by Pandit Deendayal Upadhyay some 55 years ago, in a lecture series at Mumbai. A precious principle of the structure of this philosophy was Panditji's discourse on the six enemies of humankind. Deendayalji said, 'Excessive libido, anger, greed, arrogance, temptation and jealousy are tendencies of human nature which Indian culture has called "six enemies of humankind". Such tendencies are natural and therefore when a person acts under the complete control of, say, anger or greed, that action of his is also considered natural. However, our culture teaches us that none of these negative tendencies should become fixed as part of our permanent nature. None of these should earn such prestige as to become the foundation of human nature.' All these tendencies are vices which are held in low esteem and it is possible to establish a beautiful garden of culture only if we can avoid excess of these six enemies. On the other hand, these natural tendencies become more marked in the case of animals and birds. That is why a theory like 'Might is Right' propounded by Charles Darwin takes its roots in the *jungle raj*. This is one of the central principles underlying the philosophy of Integrated Humanism of Deendayal Upadhyay.

3. George Orwell

History tells us that in the former Soviet Union, and especially during the tenure of Stalin, the bureaucracy acted completely under the spell of the six enemies of humankind. This resulted in the massacre of innumerable innocent people. That is why George Orwell, the famous British author, wrote a novel to take stock of Stalin's tenure and gave it a very appropriate title, *Animal Farm*! Coming back home, incidents from Khairlanji to Kopardi represent a wild wolf-dance of the six enemies of humankind. It is worrisome because it can reduce human beings to animals. In order to change these circumstances and encourage our society to worship the noble principles of justice and humanity, we should reinforce the social content of nationalism. This is one more reason why a deep study of the social reforms undertaken and insisted upon by Savarkar would be of great help.

4. Mahatma Phule and His Disciples

It will not be proper to speak in completely negative terms while analysing our present-day situation. This is because as stated earlier, every dark cloud has a silver lining. It will also not be fair to say that the 70 years after Independence have not produced any social reform in India. One can go back and consider the contribution of three great personalities trained and inspired by Mahatma Jyotirao Phule in the early pre-Independence period. The trinity's contribution in a way will also tell us about Jyotirao himself. The first among these three was Shivram Janba Kamble, who worked for the upliftment of the Dalits even before Dr. Babasaheb Ambedkar. The second name is that of Krishnarao Pandurang Bhalekar, who was a visionary leader who tried to bring together the farmers and artisans–the pillars of rural India. The third disciple of Jyotirao Phule was Narayan Meghaji Lokhande, who brought together industrial workers to form a union. Now imagine this if these three : Dalits, OBCs and industrial workers, awakened by these early organisers, had been united under one flag and had incessantly toiled to bring justice to the more unfortunate and underprivileged sections of the society, India would have experienced first the right order of social transformation, followed by political independence. But though this did not happen, the yeoman efforts put in by Mahatma Jyotirao Phule and his great disciples did not go waste. To some extent, due to their pioneering work, the later generation of leaders of our freedom struggle were already aware of the social core and content of nationalism. Take Raja Ram Mohan Roy or Vivekananda-Aurobindo-Lokmanya Tilak-Bipin Chandra Pal-Lala Lajpat Rai, Dayanand, Mahatma Gandhi, Savarkar, Dr. Ambedkar–all these leaders were great social reformers too. Their efforts did not remain unrewarded. All of them treated political freedom as the instrument to total resurrection of India and thus presented the same to the people. That is why the provisions related to reservation were unanimously passed by the Constitutional Assembly of India. Post-Independence, the beneficiaries of reservations numbered several hundred thousands. They could walk into the rural establishment to occupy their rightful place. This could materialise because the above-mentioned leaders had on the one hand trained the minds of upper castes while on the other, created due awareness and instilled confidence amongst Dalits, tribals/Vanvasis, OBCs and nomadic tribes.

It was in the early period of British *raj* that an officer called Stevens took the lead to get passed the Criminal

Tribes Act of 1871. And it was 81 years later, in 1952, that the Act was repealed as a result of a persistent campaign led by eminent jurists and others. Justices Iyengar and Subba Rao of Madras High Court, former Congress president Pattabhi Sitaramayya, former Governor of Bihar Durga Prasad were some of the prominent leaders who showed the sensitivity to appeal to the country's conscience against this Draconian law. This law stamped no less than 213 nomadic castes and tribes as criminals. As they were identified as crime-prone right at birth, even their children suffered from the stigma. For any crimes happening anywhere in India, these were the prime suspects to be arrested, beaten up and repeatedly imprisoned, leading to further evils, such as starvation of dependants, lack of education and of avenues of rightful earnings.

Though the Act was repealed in the country in 1952, eight more years lapsed before its effects were nullified in Maharashtra and Karnataka. At the instance of the then Chief Minister Yashwantrao Chavan, Pandit Nehru himself visited Solapur and cut the barbad wire fencing that separated the people of these tribes from the larger society. Prior to that, all those identified as criminals under the Criminal Tribes Act of 1871 had to spend their life-time within barbed-wire fencing, known as 'settlements', almost like cattle! Pandit Nehru should be given due credit for this major social reform. It is the duty of the government to respect the dignity of the citizens and to act as the guardians of the weak and the underprivileged. After the cancellation of the Act, the notified tribes were classified as Nomadic Tribes and Vimukta Jati. This brought about a new sunrise in the lives of Berad, Ramoshi, Kaikadi, Lamaan, Vadar, Kanjar Bhaat, Pardhi, Katabu, Bhamta and many other tribes.

5. Prime Minister Narendra Modi

Any government is expected to take up on its shoulders the responsibility of the people's well-being. The first BJP government, with a clear majority, was installed in Delhi in May 2014. On the Independence Day of that year, Indians got a glimpse of responsible and sensitive governance. Of course, Pandit Jawaharlal Nehru, Lal Bahadur Shastri and Atal Behari Vajpayee were also sensitive Prime Ministers. Stepping in their shoes, Narendra Modi told the audience gathered at Red Fort, 'Today we will take an oath to be ready to do our best for achieving the maximum well-being of the maximum poor, downtrodden and exploited human beings from our country.' He further said in the course of his speech, 'We should provide a variety of skill training to people who are today not doing so well. Out of them, those whom we find more enterprising should be empowered to start their own enterprises and encouraged to stand stable in the competitive urban life. They should receive the necessary aid to do this. To conclude, we should strive our best to overcome the three major challenges that we are facing, viz. upskilling, manufacturing and urbanisation.'

The background to PM Modi's speech was quite unique. In the last 10 years or so, almost 1,000 Dalit youth have established successful enterprises on their own steam. They have neither taken any benefit of caste-based reservation nor any subsidy or aid from any government or government-sponsored institution. They just made up their mind that instead of becoming job seekers, they would become job givers! Many of them succeeded in employing others! Narendra Modi now wants the same lessons to be learnt and repeated by all other backward youth so as to overcome the challenges faced by them. These thousand or so Dalit youth, who have become successful entrepreneurs, have added a completely new chapter to the book of social equality! They have founded a new apex body, named 'Dalit Indian Chamber of Commerce and Industry' (DICCI). In his prime ministerial speech on August 15th, 2014, Narendra Modi wanted to give a boost to the morale of this body and its member-youth.

Later, on December 29th, 2015, DICCI (Dalit Indian Chamber of Commerce and Industry) organised an all-India conference of Dalit entrepreneurs in New Delhi and invited Narendra Modi as the chief guest. Speaking on this occasion, Modi shared information about the schemes implemented by the BJP government for Dalit entrepreneurs. Said he, 'In the last eight months, the BJP government has provided soft loans to around 8 million people worth Rs. 50,000 crores, under MUDRA (Micro Units Development and Refinance Agency). The salient feature of this scheme is disbursement of loans without any colateral. As a result, Dalit, Vanavasi and OBC men and women were encouraged to start their own medium, small or micro enterprises. It is expected that these entrepreneurs will ultimately produce jobs for a large number of people directly or indirectly!' Modi further said in his speech, 'Reserve Bank of India of which Dr. Babasaheb Ambedkar was a sculptor, should take the initiative to persuade major Indian banks to disburse soft loans to facilitate entrepreneurship amongst the once exploited Dalits. Those youth, who inherited only poverty from their forefathers, should be encouraged to stand on their own as entrepreneurs. The foundation of the pyramid should be strengthened.' On April 5th, 2016 Modi inaugurated another initiative, 'Stand Up India', at Noida. This day was the birth anniversary of Babu Jagjivan Ram. Modi celebrated it by announcing that the government intends to provide mortgage-free loans, ranging from

Rs. 1 million to 10 million through banks to all eligible entrepreneurs coming from backward classes.

What one can observe is that the Hindu loyalists in power, fully acknowledge the social content of nationalism. That is why the government is willing to play a catalytic role in bringing up eligible members of the backward communities to blossom into successful entrepreneurs through their own efforts. These are initiatives which would really satisfy the soul of Veer Savarkar. It should be noted that in the UP assembly elections of 2017, BJP candidates got elected in 75 out of 85 reserved constituencies. This was a great morale booster for true Hindutva loyalists.

It is certain that social transformation is a long-ranging and time-consuming process. We all are taught from our childhood that everyone is a son of God and that everyone carries in his soul some divine essence. But unfortunately, we do not find this *sanskar* being practised by most people in day-to-day life. We all should remember that our culture has taught us to behave according to our *sanskars* in public as well as personal life. We should never mete out any injustice to anyone or discriminate among our brothers and sisters. Swatantryaveer Savarkar kept on preaching the same principle all his life. We too should keep making a variety of efforts to make India a heaven for just, fair and humanitarian treatment.

Savarkar came down heavily upon the concepts of high and low social status, social inequality and particularly, Untouchability. He underlined the fact that the age-old caste system had imposed seven severe restrictions on the Dalits. Said Savarkar, 'The so-called high-caste people prevent them from studying the *Vedas*. You create hindrances if they wish to do any prestigious business. You do not allow them to travel. You and your families wear ornaments made of gold and silver, but the so-called untouchable brothers and sisters can wear ornaments made only of low-grade metals. You allow your pets in your houses, but keep human beings, just like you, out of the area of your villages! And you call this religious conduct?'

Recently the United Nations defined development as an extension of freedom. Here it must be remembered that this notion was cherished by Savarkar nearly eight decades ago. He made the best of his efforts to set his Dalit brothers and sisters free from the slavery imposed on them. If we study the concept of freedom from the point of view of development, we arrive at three aspects. The *Human Development Report* of 2016 has discussed all the three aspects in an educative manner. The report says: 'If the concepts of high and low castes, inequality and untouchability are eradicated, all once-untouchables attain freedom in the true sense in such a way that they can enjoy the fruits of freedom and can utilise the freedom for self-development, the entire society can become refreshed and invigorated' (*Human Development Report 2016*, UNDP, New York, 2016).

6. Anant Hari Gadre

'Jhunka Bhakar Gadre' was an extraordinary personality.. Anant Hari Gadre was well known as the organiser of Jhunka Bhakar Satyanarayan as he asked Dalit couples to conduct the Satyanarayan *puja* in hundreds of villages. At the end of it, he would touch the feet of the host couple. That is why he was bestowed with titles, such as 'Samatanand' Gadre and 'Jhunka Bhakar' Gadre! Reputed scholar and author Dr. Sadanand More tells us that he was not only a very enterprising and active social worker, but also very sensitive too. It was his considered view from the beginning that the age-old custom of untouchability was wrong and was an evil due to which Hinduism had suffered huge setbacks. This tradition was inhuman and should be done away with. His thoughts crystallised into action due to the inspiration he received from Gandhiji, Savarkar and Sant Gadge Maharaj. He did a great deal of work almost single-handedly, due to which Kshatra Jagadguru conferred upon him the title 'Samatanand'. (Sadanand More, '*Asprushyata Nivaran Satyanarayan Prayog*', *Daily Sakal*, Pune, September 11th, 2016, p. 11).

It was a firm belief of Samatanand that the so-called high-caste Hindus had wrongly interpreted religion and imposed the evil practice of untouchability on their own brothers and sisters. Therefore, it was the duty of the high-caste Hindus to offer penance and make amends for their sin. Thus he promoted the following five principles of reforms:

1. *Sahasan* (sitting together)
2. *Sahabhojan* (eating together)
3. *Sahapoojan* (worshiping together)
4. *Sahavasan* (living together)
5. *Sahabandhan* (inter-caste marriage)

Out oſ the several activities that he conducted, the 'jhunka bhakar Satyanarayan' *puja* proved to be very innovative and effective. Normally for such a *puja*, one requires costly edible items like pure *ghee* and sugar. But how could the poor Dalits afford them? So Samatanand Gadre presented to them the option of performing the *puja* with simple, inexpensive *jhunka* and *bhakari* to serve as *naivedya* and *prasad* (offerings to God)! Pandit Panse Shastri prepared a revised scripture for the *puja*. The most important change brought about by Gadre was that the host couple performing the *puja* had to be from the so-called untouchable castes. At the end of the *puja*, Gadre would himself wash the feet of the host couple and drink that water, treating it as *teerth* or holy water. While drinking it, he would recite a slightly revised *shloka* (couplet):

समाजमृत्युहरणं जातिद्वेषनिवारणं।
हरिजनपादोदकं तीर्थं जठरे धारयाम्यहम्।।

(I am now going to drink the holy water emanating from the feet of the Dalit/Harijan for the purpose of obliterating communal dislike and saving our society from an untimely death!)

This Sanskrit couplet was improvised from the original *shloka* which is recited after completing the *yogic* exercise of Surya Namaskar. Here is the original:

अकालमृत्युहरणं सर्वव्याधिविनाशनं।
सूर्यपादोदकं तीर्थं जठरे धारयाम्यहम्।।

This is for worshipping Sun-god but the improvised one is meant to uphold the need to end untouchability. Whenever a Dalit couple would complete performing the *puja*, Samatanand Gadre would recite the improvised couplet and actually drink a few drops of the water with which he washed the host couple's feet. This was the extent of his sincerity to the cause. When joint lunches were arranged for the so-called upper caste and lower-caste Hindus, Veer Savarkar would also utter a revised line to mark the beginning of the lunch : 'अखिल हिंदू सहभोजनं करिष्ये' (let us all Hindus break bread together). Both these steps were revolutionary indeed, considering the conventional tenor of that period. These steps were valuable for changing social attitudes. Dr. Ambedkar and others took due cognisance of Savarkar's contribution in the field of initiating social transformation.

7. Dr. Ambedkar's Appreciation for Savarkar

During the period of house arrest of Savarkar at Ratnagiri, Dr. Ambedkar organised the famous *satyagraha* at *Chavadar Taley* (Tasty Water Lake) in Mahad, Maharashtra. Another *satyagraha* was organised at Nashik for allowing entry to the untouchables into the famous Kala Ram Mandir. It was led by Bhaurao Gaikwad. Savarkar could not join these *satyagrahas* due to restrictions on his movement, but he wrote letters to leaders of the so-called high-caste Hindus at Mahad and Nashik, requesting them in the name of justice to accept the demands of the untouchables. Of course, he was already doing a lot of work in Ratnagiri district for the eradication of untouchability. Dr. Babasaheb Ambedkar praised the work done by Savarkar in these words: 'I am taking this opportunity of appreciating the work being done by you in the field of social reforms. If the so-called untouchable class has to be a part of the Hindu society, eradication of untouchability is a must, but is not adequate. We should completely uproot the concept of *chaturvarnya*. I am glad that you are one of the few who are convinced about its necessity' (Dhananjay Keer, *Swatantryaveer Savarkar*, p. 202).

8. Tarkateerth Lakshmanshastri Joshi, Vitthal Ramji Shinde and Madhavrao Bagal

Savarkar brought about a social revolution in Ratnagiri district during the 13-year period of his house arrest for which he was praised by many leading thinkers of Maharashtra. Tarkateerth Lakshmanshastri Joshi said, 'Savarkar fought against the age-old traditions and customs with the sword of rationalism. He had realised that the only way to strengthen the Hindu society was to completely obliterate the unholy symptoms of blind faith, casteism and superstitions!' Bhai Madhavrao Bagal and Karmveer Vitthal Ramji Shinde were unusually impressed by the work done by Savarkar. Maharshi Shinde wrote a poem, praying to God that his remaining life should be credited to Savarkar! Madhavrao Bagal said, "It is difficult to gather 5 to 10 women in big cities like Pune or Mumbai for a joint lunch. In Kolhapur, we have just not been able to do it, but in Ratnagiri, hundreds of women came together for such a lunch. This is a social revolution and its credit goes to Tatyarao Savarkar! (References from the book by Dr. Ramesh Kamble).

9. Uttam Kamble

Journalist, author and editor Uttam Kamble informs the readers thus: 'In case of backward and nomadic tribes like Pardhi, changes happened on different levels, once they started following the path of development. Pardhi families started naming their children differently. In the past, in many nomadic tribes, newly-born children were given names like Pistulya, Bandookya, Kothadya, Lutya, Remand and the like! Once they came out of the barbed-wire settlements, these families started naming their children normally like Arun, Komal, Suresh, Siddharth, Samvidhan, Adhikar, Bheemrav and the like. In the last few years, you will find several youth from communities like Pardhi, Kudmudya Joshi and Vadar have taken a big leap forward to reach the posts of government officers by being selected on merit. The society can change, but someone has to cause the change. Gautam Buddha had rightly pointed out that inspirations behind human existence keep on changing.' (Uttam Kamble, '*Pistulya te Samvidhan*', *Sakal*, Pune, September 11th, 2016, p. 16).

10. Sanjay Paswan

'All this while the backward castes were instigated to constantly oppose the forward castes and in this way, people and parties in power tried to patronise the lower castes. This politicisation of the issues of caste system is now failing. Social inequality and the notions of higher and lower castes have remained unbeaten. In addition, some sub-castes from the backward classes have taken undue advantages of the system. The conclusion is that in the field of social reforms, outreach and patronage, both are not beneficial to the common people. The politics of outrage and patronage has run its course.' This is the considered opinion expressed by Sanjay Paswan, former Union Minister (Sanjay Paswan, 'A New Dalit Agenda', *The Indian Express*, Mumbai, May 5th, 2017, p. 12).

□

24

The Hindu Unity Song

Thus Spoke Swatantryaveer Savarkar...

Savarkar wrote the poem, *The Hindu Unity Song* (*Hindunche Ekatagaan* in Marathi) with an extremely engaging refrain. It reads as follows:

तुम्हि–आम्ही सकल हिंदू बंधुबंधु।
तो महादेवजी पिता आपुला चला तया वंदू।।

Savarkar was confident that we will be able to overcome a number of outdated customs and traditions, if we consider ourselves as Hindus, if we have a generous attitude and are large-hearted rather than being satisfied within the narrow compounds of castes and sub-castes. The very first stanza of this poem directly attacks the practice of casteism:

ब्राह्मण वा क्षत्रिय चांग। जरी झाला।
कसलेहि रूप वा रंग। जरि ल्याला।
तो महार अथवा मांग। सकलांला।
ही एकचि आहे हिंदूजाति आम्हा तिला वंदू।।

(Whether a human being was born a Brahmin or a Kshatriya or in any other caste, he's our brother because we worship only one mother: Hinduism!)

Current Situation and Analysis

Savarkar found the practice of untouchability a curse.

He decided to eradicate it along with other bans like restrictions on studying scriptures, freedom of profession, eating together, inter-caste marriage, re-conversion to Hinduism and travel across the oceans. He was optimistic of convincing his countrymen against these social evils and their adverse effects on the society. That is why during his long stay at Ratnagiri, he wrote literature that expressed his convictions. His poem titled 'The Hindu Unity Song', composed in 1925 also reconfirmed his convictions.

Seniors' Views

Comrade Hiren Mukherjee delivered a series of lectures on Dr. Babasaheb Ambedkar in New Delhi. While concluding the lecture series, he recited a Sanskrit *shloka* besides giving his commentary on it. The *shloka* stands as follows:

माता मे पार्वती देवी।
पिता देवो महेश्वर:।
बांधवा: मानवा: सर्वे।
स्वदेशो भुवनत्रयम्।।

(Parvati Devi is my mother and Bhagwan Shiva is my father. All human beings are my brothers and my country represents all that is there in the world and beyond!)

Hiren Mukherjee said that we should always remember this *shloka* and work towards removing social inequality and notions of high and low castes in the light of this *shloka*.

Much before Comrade Mukherjee delivered this lecture, Savarkar had composed the 'Hindu Unity Song' in 1925. Its refrain contained a line having the same meaning : that Bhagwan Shiva is our father! Thus the original Sanskrit shloka that Savarkar had in front of him while composing his song was also remembered by Comrade Hiren Mukherjee, when delivering his speech on Dr. Ambedkar. He also did not feel any compunction in explaining its meaning to the audience. This shows that Savarkar and Mukherjee subscribed to the same cultural heritage, the same religious traditions and the same belief that social evils can be eradicated in the light of a common past glory. Savarkar and Mukherjee shared this conviction in spite of contradictory political views. But they both were on the same page regarding removal of social inequality, the inspiration for which will come from Lord Shiva and not from Marx. In other words, India's complex problems cannot be solved by quoting complex theories of 'Base and Superstructure Thesis'. They can be resolved only by connecting with the common cultural heritage that we share. We can bury our differences if we realise that we have a common cultural past. This is the eternal truth. We should remember that after a passage of 80 years, the ideas and ideals of Marx, Lenin and Stalin are fading into oblivion whereas the basic thought of Savarkar is receiving support from all over the country.

Dalit Youth as Temple Priests

It was in Diwali of 2017 that the mass media gave pleasant news, one which would have pleased the soul of Savarkar. He always held this conviction that all Hindus are brothers of each other with equal status. Against this background, a sort of social revolution was created in Kerala, in 2017, when the Travancore Devaswom Board appointed five Dalit youth as priests in their temples. *Times of India* of October 18th, 2017 carried the interview of one of the young priests, named P.K. Yadu Krishna who was excited to be welcomed as a priest. "I have now become a priest in Mahadev Mandir at Thiruvalla. This has been welcomed by all organisations and parties. This is the sweet fruit of the movement started by Sri Narayana Guru for social transformation.' That is a social revolution that respectfully greeted Veer Savarkar 54 years after he laid down his life!

□

25

Development is Expansion of Freedom

Thus Spoke Swatantryaveer Savarkar...

Veer Savarkar was arrested in March 1910 in the city of London. The charges levelled against him were very severe and Savarkar was aware that he was liable to receive an excessively harsh punishment. So he decided to write a letter to his respected and dear sister-in-law Yesu Vahini to apprise her of the future arrangements. The poetic letter that he wrote to her was titled 'My Will' (*Maze Mrutyupatra* in Marathi). Two lines from this letter are worth quoting:

दीप्तानलात निज-मातृ-विमोचनार्थ।
हा स्वार्थ जाळुनी अम्ही ठरलो कृतार्थ।।

(It was necessary to ignite a sacred fire for the sake of Independence of our motherland. We sacrificed our selfish interests in it and have now become chaste and gratified.)

Current Situation and Analysis

Veer Savarkar's entire life was a life of sacrifice. Such selfless noble deeds won Independence for India. It is now our holy duty to do our very best to convert *swarajya* into *surajya,* based on the principles of equality and affection.

The *UN Report* of 2016 has given an explanation of intrinsic, instrumental and constructive aspects of individual freedom, but how great a visionary Savarkar was that during his 13-year period at Ratnagiri (1924-1937), he began to practise what he preached while paying the heavy price of public censure by upper-caste Hindus.

If a human being is set free from years of captivity, can you really measure his happiness? If someone who was imprisoned in a dark dungeon for years together was freed to enjoy open climate, breeze and sunlight, others cannot imagine the extent of his intinsic pleasure. Now if this former prisoner undertakes a profession, earns well and enjoys a high standard of living, he will be blessed with an active pleasure of freedom. Imagine a socio-cultural eco-system wherein nobody is untouchable or downtrodden, where all are privileged to walk the path of progress in unison... how much positive energy will this climate generate in the society! That is the constructive enjoyment of independence.

Once India achieved Independence, its Constituent Assembly legislated social welfare measures, such as a ban on untouchability and reservation for the underprivileged. Veer Savarkar welcomed these constitutional measures in a public discourse.

The *United Nations Human Development Report* of 2016 has expressed the view that such welfare-oriented provisions are desirable in order to transform a representative democracy into participative democracy. This report also offers excellent clarification about how different sections of the society should behave for the success of participative democracy. It is a fact that development is an expansion or extended form of independence. However, on the one hand, the deprived, depressed or underprivileged sections of the society should utilise this freedom to become happy and enriched by the strength of their own deeds, whereas the higher social strata, which is already privileged should be aware of its duty to utilise freedom for the welfare and benefit of the underprivileged. This is their *Karmayog*. The *Report* expresses this in the following words:

'People may thus volunteer for causes that do not advance their own well-being, such as protecting the rights or improving the conditions of vulnerable groups or conserving ecosystems, landmarks or historical monuments. People may put themselves in gruelling situations, working to promote causes they believe in at the cost of their own health or security.'

During his stay at Ratnagiri, Swatantryaveer Savarkar undertook a variety of projects and activities to achieve broader society-oriented objectives. He did all this at the cost of his personal pleasure. He also encouraged his colleagues, most of whom belonged to the so-called upper castes, to go through such gruelling and demanding activities in a selfless manner. Due to such concentrated efforts of Savarkar and his colleagues, Ratnagiri district was blessed with social transformation and development much before attaining political Independence.

In the year 2016, the world started moving towards attainment of sustainable human development. Was it not an extraordinary coincidence that we celebrated the 50th death anniversary of Veer Savarkar that very year?

□□□